REACHING FOR JUSTICE:

The Women's Movement

Mary P. Burke

To my parents Anna Folen Burke
and Edward Burke whose dreams
are being harvested by their children
and grandchildren.

CONTENTS

INTRODUCTION

Under normal circumstances, Mexico City is an imagination-stretching blend of old and new. Women wrapped in shawls or dressed in the latest fashions move alongside men in baggy work clothes and two-piece suits on traffic-filled streets that link restored Indian structures and modern steel and concrete office buildings. On the morning of June 19, 1975, the scene exploded with new colors and styles as over 5,000 women hurried to the opening of the United Nations sponsored World Conference of the International Women's Year.

Seated high in the stands of the *Gimnasio Juan de la Barrera* I noticed that the eyes of my companion were as wide as her grin. My expression must have matched hers. Before us, women from 133 countries hurried to seats in the large stadium. Africans in brilliant tie-dyed dresses walked next to Filipinas in pastel-colored butterfly-sleeved dresses. Indians in airy, embroidered saris stood next to Chinese in dark blue jackets and trousers. It seemed like a dream, but it wasn't. Along with 4999 other women I was at the Women's Conference.

In 1974, the Center of Concern initiated its project, Women in Church and Society: A Call to Justice. The project team, Jane Blewett, Sister Elizabeth Caroll, RSM, Rev. William F. Ryan, S.J., and I, set the 1975 International Women's Year (IWY) Conference as our first focus. We originally planned to examine two topics: women and socio-economic development in the Third World and women in the Catholic Church. We studied the issues before the Mexico City Conference and examined questions raised by women in the Church. We prepared memoranda and talks on our findings. In addition, we quickly learned that 1) the issues involved much more than we had imagined and 2) we could not deal with either of these two areas without facing the concerns of women in the United States.

After the IWY Conference the project's basic thrust was continued, with modifications. We began incorporating some of the key justice issues that were on the domestic agenda. As we came to better understand the Equal Rights Amendment, as well as the actual legal protections women had, for example, we became ERA advocates.

We also devoted more of our energy to identifying and exploring the links between the issues facing women in the United States and women in the developing countries. We quickly came to see that worldwide women's economic (productive), as opposed to child bearing and homemaking (reproductive), activities are overlooked. Furthermore, whether in the United States or in Bangladesh, most women struggle to find ways to earn money to meet their own needs and those of their families. The manner in which these factors impact the lives of women are significantly different in the Third World and the U.S.—different enough to make similarities seem trivial. Yet these issues serve as one of the bonds among women around the world.

Research and consultation support our judgment that religion is a significant element in the lives of most women. In 1976 as part of the women's project, the Center sponsored the Women, Religion, and Development Conference. The meeting was small enough for everyone to participate in yet had representatives from all five world religions and every part of the world. It raised questions about the relationships between women and religion that are still being answered.

The women's project team has changed since 1974. Both Sister Betty Carroll and Father Bill Ryan have left the Center of Concern. Sister Maria Riley, O.P. has joined the team. Joseph Holland, Fathers Peter Henriot, S.J., and Philip Land, S.J. have at times contributed their efforts and insights.

This publication is another step in the project's growth. It is time, the team feels, to set the women's movement in context, to pull together the thinking on some issues, to reflect on emerging issues and to bring new insights to older issues. We hope it will encourage women who have been watchers to become active participants in the continuing dialogue about women's situations and roles.

A Personal Note

When we began to explore the possibility of a women's project at the Center of Concern it was logical that I should have a part in it. My work at the Center had increased my awareness of the injustices faced by women in both the Church and the larger society. The prospect of participating in the United Nations International Women's Year activities lent added excitement to the project. If, however, even two years earlier someone had predicted I would spend much time on women's issues, I would have shaken my head in denial. As a single, lay woman, I have lived with injustices that women face, yet like many others, I have been slow to recognize the importance of these issues. I have been even slower in acknowledging my involvement in this movement for change.

In 1967, after eight years of high school teaching and four years as a copy editor of a scientific journal, I entered the University of Connecticut as a full-time graduate student in political science. By 1970 the women's movement was an active presence on the campus, but it was not my issue. The Viet Nam conflict, fairer and more reasonable treatment of graduate students, and the general effort to create a more just society occupied my "free" time.

Those six years I spent at the University of Connecticut were for me a time of personal as well as intellectual growth. Looking back, I realize that I was also becoming involved in the women's movement. It did not take long for me to realize that the faculty of fifteen to twenty men and one woman treated me differently from the other women students. They assumed that because I was over 30 and unmarried I was "serious" about my studies. Younger women, especially recent graduates, had their "seriousness" constantly tested even though they were often better students than their male counterparts. (Some of the latter drifted into and through graduate school in those years of the Viet Nam draft.)

The women's group on campus raised questions to the whole university community. I found myself raising questions within my department. "No, I'm not a part of the women's movement but..." was the start of more than one discussion. Friends made me aware of emerging questions, and I passed on what I learned. I absorbed a lot from the movement I didn't belong to.

Nevertheless, my transition from "I'm not a part of the women's movement" to "yes, I'm working for women's liberation" has been uneven and awkward. It has been fearfilled and painful as well as strengthening and exhilarating.

Many times the questions and analysis I applied to women's situations have become personal questions. I am no longer engaged in an academic exercise; my response affects the way I view myself and my relationship with others. Aware of the impact of sexist language, for example, I find that it distracts me from what is being said, even when I make a conscious effort to hear beyond it (liturgy is one example). Sometimes, sexist language makes me so angry that I spend time dealing with my anger, instead of doing what I'm supposed to be doing.

The world undervalues women's work. Do other women? Do I? How must I change my attitude, behavior and response to homemakers, for example, so that I do not continue to participate in this injustice? How much of my beliefs about women and my values are based upon sexist conditioning? How do I relate to sexist institutions? These questions and others must be answered again and again as I learn more about sexism. And like many other women I must constantly watch for that fine line between a) separating the truly human values which are essential to being a Christian and a whole person from the practices and beliefs of a culture that is deeply biased against women and b) destroying the values themselves. As I try to shape answers, I have come to appreciate the importance of a support community.

3

Because I am involved with the women's movement, I am challenged by some who see the struggle for justice for women as a distraction from the bigger fight against injustice and poverty. At first I responded defensively. Now, I realize that the challenge is a distraction. The poorest people in the United States and throughout the world are women and their children.

Rosemary Ruether has suggested an approach to some of the world's evils that makes sense to me. She classifies the injustices of our time as classism, racism, sexism, and a disregard for the earth. Very few of us can effectively work on all four issues—I cannot. But as we focus our energies on one or another of these injustices, Prof. Ruether urges us to keep all four and their relationships in mind. This understanding helps me as I meet challenges to my choice of struggling for women. I believe that there is a way to battle against sexism and at the same time undermine other injustices.

The process of writing *Reaching for Justice: The Women's Movement* has been a process of renewed commitment. I've read and listened, and been forced to clarify my thoughts. I've come to realize once again both the pervasiveness of sexism and the importance of overcoming it.

This Book

I began writing with three goals: 1) setting the U.S. women's movement in context, 2) analyzing the factors that shape some of the basic issues facing the movement and in the process 3) answering some of the questions of women who are ambivalent toward or puzzled by the movement. I have used the term "women's movement" to mean that overall endeavor to secure justice for women, not just the organizations that are a part of that effort. The Equal Rights Amendment, the development of a global perspective, and the relationship between the women's movement and the family and religion are key issues for women at this time. Much attention has been given to the changes in the interrelationships among structures, particularly socio-economic structures and the situation and roles of majority of women. Less attention has been given to personal relationships and the emotional bonds that enrich life.

This study is only a beginning, a *primer*. Each of the topics chosen deserves far more attention than it receives in the chapters below. The stress on socio-economics has meant that cultural aspects of discrimination have not been probed and examined as they need to be. It has also meant that other factors, those that humanize life and balance the impact of societal structures, have not been adequately examined.

This study is incomplete in another aspect. The stories of minority women, Asian, black, Hispanic, and native American women, have not been examined. The structures that shape the lives of majority women form the lives of these women as well. To an extent, then, this study begins to tell their story. But because they bear the weight of racism as well as those of sexism and classism, there are qualitative differences in their lives. These differences have not been probed in this work.

Despite these limits, I think *Reaching for Justice: The Women's Movement* is a start toward achieving the original goals. If it helps move the discussion along, if it opens the way to exploring issues with new insights, I'll feel it is successful.

Many people helped with this book. They each deserve my thanks. When I began writing I asked some people to act as experts and critics. They read chapter drafts and sent back comments. I appreciate the time and thought given by Eileen Dooley, Barbara Gieskes, Joris Gieskes, Dana Green, Judy Justinger, Judy Murray and Julie Zito. Other people read a chapter, or talked out an idea and I am grateful for their insights and interest. The staff of the Center of Concern, Jane Blowett, Peter Henriot, S.J., Joe Holland, Philip Land, S.J., and Maria Riley, O.P., and Anne Stygles not only read and critiqued but listened with patience as I thought out loud, set deadlines that weren't met and grumbled. Lucinda Williams has played as special role as first reader and typist. Without all of this support this book would not have been written. In the end, though, what is written is my responsibility. Only I can be held to account for what is said, not said, or said inadequately.

1.
THE SETTING FOR A WOMEN'S MOVEMENT: WOMEN'S STORY

As a young woman, I shared with my friends a vision of the good life that served as a standard for us. That vision and the reality did not fit together well, so we had questions about both, including some about the proper role and place of women. Today, with the rise of the women's movement, these questions are commanding the attention of many more people.

With few exceptions, most Americans acknowledge the claim that women in our society and elsewhere bear injustices. We keep asking, however, just where do the injustices lie? Are women's demands excessive? Are they contributing to today's social disruption? And, probably most important of all, how do we create a just situation for women, one that respects the gifts of individual women, yet preserves our valuable institutions such as the family, and creates a more human society for all?

A part of the answer lies in questioning the myths we have about women's lives. To do that we must step back and look at how women's position and roles in society have evolved as society itself has changed.

The Roots of Our Myths: Pre-Industrial Society

The ideas many of us have about a good life have been built in part on a memory of society before industrialization. History and myth tell us that in the past there was a wholeness about life that is missing now. Families remained close together and members shared and cared for each other. Children were cared for by aunts and grandmothers as well as mothers. Education took place in the home or a home-like setting, and the whole family had important roles in the process. Neighbors and those who worked together felt a responsibility for each other, cared for those in need and celebrated together the joys of life. The pace of life was controlled by the seasons, thus there were times of intense work and long periods of rest. There was, moreover, a basic agreement about the meaning of life, how the society should operate, and how benefits and responsibilities should be distributed.

We know, but have not built into our myths, other aspects of this period. Life was harsh, often cruel. Life expectancy was short. Poor health conditions and disease meant that more children died than survived. Everyone had a part in producing the goods and services needed to keep the family and the community functioning. Even so, clothing, farm tools, medicine, and most of the goods we take for granted were scarce. The poor (most people) had little to share. Food itself was often at a premium. Few roads and poor communications meant that when a crop failed, food would not be shifted to feed the hungry. People moved or starved. Roving bands of women as well as men were not uncommon.

Women's Place in Pre-Industrial Society

The basic agreements on how society should operate included agreements on women's proper roles. Like the society itself, women were divided by class: peasants, guild workers, members of religious communities or members of the aristocracy. By definition and in practice they were, class notwithstanding, inferior beings, possessions of their fathers or husbands with little control over their own lives.

Peasant women (most women) worked in the fields, maintained home gardens, cared for chickens and farm animals, prepared food for storage and consumption, made fabric and then the family's clothing. They did all this while bearing and nursing children and seeing to their family's day to day needs.

Women in guild workshops experienced what was to become the model for most women with the coming of industrialization. A few guilds, such as embroidering, millinery, silk, and so forth, were all-women guilds whose members received all the training necessary to become experts in their craft. In most instances, however, women received some training but not enough to become master craftpersons. Nevertheless, their help was indispensable for the effective operation of the workshop. There were many reasons why women remained helpers rather than experts: they were less free to travel as journeymen than men because they had children to care for; their household responsibilities cut into their work time; and most lacked the physical strength needed for some tasks, such as smithing. More important, however, seems to be the view that there were many things, such as making household utensils or shoes, that women couldn't do or shouldn't do. A few women did carry out these restricted jobs and carried them out well. Some widows, for instance, successfully managed their husband's workshops. These exceptions, though, did not change people's minds about what women could do.

For both peasant and guild worker, life lacked security. Leisure was a luxury. Though men's work might lighten in the winter, women's did not (spinning and weaving supplemented field work, for example). The large, healthy family that lightened the household burdens in good times often disintegrated in the face of economic adversity. At those times, young women, teenagers, even pre-teens, as well as young men and boys, moved from home, the former to become servants or apprentices. They were then subject to harassment and responsible for any children they might have. Widows had few rights or protections. With their young children, they were often forced off the land or out of the workshop.

The other significant option open to women was that of a spiritually-oriented life in a community. Religious orders were organized under the direction of a priest or bishop who set the rule for most details of women's daily activity. Less common were secular institutes where women lived a spiritual yet more independent life. One example of the latter was the Beguines, common in parts of Western Europe from the 12th to the 14th Century. These communities of pious women set up their own workshops, and sheltered the most needy women and children. Some of these women, as well as members of religious orders, became advisors to priests, bishops, and government leaders.

One group of women, a small minority, had a different set of opportunities through this period. Female members of families of the aristocracy and intelligentsia had a life of relative comfort. Nevertheless, women of the manor houses were as busy as poorer women. They had responsibility for the preparation and preservation of a great volume of agricultural and craft products. These women supervised the operation of large households that in effect served as small, multi-purpose factories for the countryside.

A very small number of women had an education and sometimes social responsibilities that compared favorably with their brothers and husbands. Queens such as Isabel of Spain and Elizabeth I of England and scholar/artists such as Beatriz Galindo of Spain, Marie de Jan de Gaurnay of France, and Anna Maria Ardain of Italy were few in number and had opportunities for public life that were rarely open to women. They were not models for other women but did demonstrate that given resources and opportunity women were as capable as men.

The United States Experience

Although industrialization was well underway in Europe while the United States was being settled, agriculture dominated this nation's early life. In many ways rural life in the U.S. was similar to that of Europe: men and women worked together; work was hard and the pleasures much appreciated; although the pace of life changed with the seasons, women had little leisure time.

There were important differences between life in Europe and the United States as well. Three are worth noting here. First, class divisions in the United States, although significant, were neither as sharp or rigid as in Europe. Instead racial divisions became prominent as skin color became a reason for discrimination that still exists. Second, farmhouses were not clustered in villages but rather spread across the countryside. The isolation that was a part of farm life encouraged independence and self-reliance, traits still important to us.

Finally, settler women, whether living in the east in the 17th Century or in the west in the 19th Century, usually lived a freer life than the ordinary social conventions allowed. There was little choice in this matter. If families were to survive, wives had to be able to manage their surroundings as well as husbands did. Thus, women on isolated farms could shoot and handle machinery and livestock as well as run a household. Many became the family bookkeeper and manager, sharing decision-making with their spouses. Others, such as widows, or the spouses of trappers, traders, or soldiers had full responsibility for family survival. This heritage is just now being publicized. It promises us models of women of courage, self-confidence, and accomplishment.

Change as the Only Constant: Industrialized Society

Industrialization, slowly yet profoundly, has changed every aspect of life over the last few hundred years. It brought people off the land into towns and then cities. This changed the way people organized their daily life and related to each other. The amount of goods available increased to meet the demands of a growing population and in time became accessible to a greater proportion of the population. Increased demands for food led to more efficient agricultural practice which led to greater, if uneven, productivity.

The concentration of people and the demands of industry and agriculture stimulated the arts and sciences. New areas of learning developed as scholars examined one or another aspects of life.

Newer and better methods of communication made the new knowledge and ideas a part of the popular culture. Many activities such as education and health care, once linked to the household, became professionalized.

The structural changes and technology that have been a part of the industrialization process have varied with geography, class, and race. Women living in urban areas have had their lives shaped more immediately by shifts in the costs and benefits of industrial growth than rural women. Class and race have been important in determining whether costs or benefits have had the greater impact. In the end, however, the structure of every woman's life has been formed by industrialization.

At the close of the Civil War, the United States was well on the way to becoming the industrial nation it is today. Since then many of our ideas about women, especially those about appropriate roles and behavior, have been shaped and reshaped as the society has responded to the consequences of industrialization and economic growth. The rest of this chapter will look at some of these changes with particular attention to the areas of education, work within and outside the home, including child care, and myths about women's proper roles. Although the focus will be on urban women, these same changes influenced the lives of rural women as well.

A Society in Transition: 1865-1915

The Middle Class

By the 1860s a significant number of Americans were neither poor nor wealthy. They were a part of the growing American middle class. Successful businessmen, doctors, lawyers, and other professionals, managers, clergy, skilled craftsmen, some of the better paid clerks, and other workers saw themselves as middle class. They felt they had escaped poverty and had some choice about where they would live and how they would spend their income.

Extensive industrialization and urbanization expanded the size of this group unevenly but steadily from 1870 onward. The income spread and standard of living varied greatly between those just managing and those who formed the upper middle class. Yet there was, as there is today, elements of a commonly accepted life style. Men expected to be the sole family wage-earners. Women expected to be full-time homemakers. The family's economic situation did not depend upon the earnings of offspring, thus, children could at least complete high school. The term family came to mean nuclear family as the cohesiveness of the extended family lessened. Larger homes, more elaborate clothing that needed to be kept cleaned and ironed, and a more sophisticated taste in food made substantial demands on homemakers. Large families meant that a woman's day was long. The workload was reduced in upper-income families by domestic servants. Initially, newly freed black women, then immigrants, were a ready source of domestic help. Later as the supply of servants decreased, labor-saving appliances cut the time required for some tasks.

■ Child Care

During the last decade of the 1800s children and child rearing became the objects of close study as scholars and medical doctors began to examine the physical, intellectual, and moral growth of children. Books and magazines popularized research findings and the experts' opinions. Heavy responsibility was placed on women for the future success and happiness of their children. Women were told that they had to be attentive to all aspects of children's development: failings of a child were due to failings of the mother. The wise mother was defined as the woman who kept herself informed and consulted the experts when she had any questions.

Great stress was placed on the need for proper moral training. It was felt that women with their special gifts of gentleness and firmness could provide this training—provided they themselves were properly trained. Cooperation between home and school, assuring mutual supervision of child rearing, became standard. Mothers' Clubs fostered this cooperation. By 1910, a nationwide network of Mothers' Clubs, the National Congress of Mothers, had 50,000 members anxious to learn more about mothering and enjoyed a good bit of political clout. The Congress promoted kindergartens and their public funding as well as legislation improving the situation of poor women and children (in 1924 this organization became the Parents Teachers Association).

■ The Image of Women

The rather strenuous responsibilities women had were in sharp contrast to what one might expect. Conventional wisdom held that women were weak and fragile, especially susceptible to emotional disorders. They were particularly vulnerable during menstruation as well as pregnancy, and while nursing. It was believed that young women should not be faced with serious education or employment demands, because any harm that might result would affect their childbearing abilities and future health.

■ Education

Concern for the health of young women was one argument used to defeat efforts to provide young women with the opportunity for college education prior to 1865 (see Chapter 2 for details). In that year Vassar College was founded as the first college for women. In an effort to counter the anxiety about women's health, Vassar's first curriculum incorporated an extensive physical education program. The predicted health problems did not materialize. Soon Vassar was followed by other women's colleges and the physical education requirement of that original curriculum was reduced.

Education, especially higher education, for women was justified in terms of women's roles as child nurturers and homemakers. College education, it was argued, prepared women to be wives of business and professional men. More importantly, it prepared them to meet the increasingly complex demands of motherhood. Most educated young women happily accepted this argument. Yet once educated, many did not confine all their energies to the household.

Access to higher education enabled women to participate more fully in intellectual and civic life as the 19th Century ended and the 20th Century began. Child development was only one of the new disciplines that emerged. Concern for the problems facing urban societies, the need for greater agricultural productivity, and the search for better and cheaper industrial production stimulated research, and efforts to publicize that research. The social sciences became an important part of the college curriculum and in women's colleges these courses often gave significant attention to the negative impact of industrial and urban life on the poor. Women found outlets for their new knowledge in two spheres: clubs and employment.

■ Women's Clubs

Whether or not they accepted the image of frailty, many middle-class women also carried another image of themselves. They believed they were morally and spiritually superior to men and to the poor, and that they had the responsibility to reform society or at least guard the good in it. Sheila Rothman in her study of women and public policy, *Women's Proper Place,* points out that women's clubs became vehicles for educating women and enabling them to promote the common good. City women, worried about the well-being of young farm girls seeking work in the city, established the YWCA in 1866. The Women's Christian Temperance Union, founded in 1873, began its drive against taverns and liquor and for women's right to vote. Bellevue School of Nursing was founded in 1873 by the female-dominated New York State Charities Aid Association in an effort to better hospitals and hospital care.

Thirty years later these middle- and upper-class women and their ideas were a part of the social and political mainstream. The United

States were passing through a period of legal and social reforms since labeled the Progressive Era (1898-1917). Past efforts at creating a better society began to succeed. Sanitation, health care, and basic health knowledge began to improve. More babies lived beyond infancy, more women survived childbirth, and lifespans grew longer. New efforts were undertaken: the campaign to insure the quality of food reaching the market led to the Pure Food and Drug Act of 1906.

Concern about child development led to attempts to restrict the kind and length of employment open to children. These attempts were substantially successful in urban areas by 1916, four years after the establishment of the Children's Bureau. Settlement houses, founded in urban slums with the aims of introducing college women to urban life and helping immigrants become Americans, developed significant programs for children especially in the fields of recreation, education, and health. Finally, concern for children and the family was one of the strong arguments used in promoting legislation to limit the hours and kinds of work women could do. A woman who was overtired or in ill health because of poor working conditions could not, it was argued, properly care for her family, her most important responsibility.

In all these efforts, club women, educated by the new colleges and women's magazines, played an important role. They were publicists and motivators for change. In addition, many served in the settlement houses and other agencies that provided services.

■ Work Outside the Home

Many young women, especially those from middle-class families just managing, took advantage of the employment opportunities that continually expanded after 1865. Teaching, especially primary school teaching, had by 1890 become the domain of women. A Normal School education prepared women for the job for which all agreed they were well suited. The rise of department stores required a new kind of sales clerk, one who was properly dressed and mannerly. For some middle-class and more working-class girls this was an ideal position.

With the development of the typewriter in 1874 office work became the province of young women. A high school education meant a girl could spell and punctuate properly and she was welcomed in the office. Although teaching, spelling, and typing were quite different jobs, they did have characteristics in common. The pay for women was low in comparison to what men received in the same position. It was claimed that women did not need or want more than the income necessary to take care of their immediate cost of living. In each of these instances, supervision was carried out by men who were paid substantially higher wages. Their tasks included enforcing behavior and dress codes as well as insuring that the women did their work.

The expansion of social services through settlement houses and similar institutions after 1890 expanded the employment opportunities for college-educated women. There was need for social workers, nutritionists, public health nurses, and teachers who could train immigrant and poor women to better care for their children. Other women found work as writers and lecturers who popularized then current progressive ideas. Most of the positions open to middle-class women were open to young women. It was assumed that women would marry and then withdraw to their homes. There were some exceptions to this assumption. Not all women married and thus they found themselves permanent members of the work force. As early as 1888, for example, 34 percent of the women working in the Columbus, Ohio, school system had worked for 19 years or more; most were unmarried.

There were few if any openings for married women who for whatever reasons wanted to rejoin the work force. This absence of employment opportunities created difficulties for middle-class women as it did for their working-class contemporaries. Insurance and pensions were scarce for most of these families. Business failures could cost the family all its assets. For middle-class women who needed an income, taking in sewing was acceptable, as was preparing preserves, baked goods and fine sewing for the Women's Exchange or giving music or elocution lessons.

However, popular magazines and books such as Ellen Church's *Money Making for Ladies* said that no one was supposed to know a woman was earning money. The reality, of course, was different: when disaster struck, vulnerable middle-class families became working-class or poor in a very short time. And many women had no alternative but to become self-supporting.

The Working Class

By the end of the Civil War the promise of work and a better life attracted native born and immigrants alike to the growing cities. The life many, especially immigrants, actually found was hard and insecure; the line between poverty and destitution was very narrow.

Wages were low, often not meeting family living costs. Unemployment was common—the census of 1900 reported six and one-half million people out of work. One consequence was that wives as well as husbands and older children often worked outside the home. Housing itself was cramped. It was not uncommon for families to share apartments or rent out rooms. M.E. Ravage, a

Rumanian immigrant, tells of the transformation each evening of a five-room apartment into a "camp" for 12 or more in *An American in the Making*.

Family life under these circumstances meant struggle and sacrifice. For many women, even for those who did not contribute to the family income, new tasks were added to old. It was important, for example, that children in school and many workers present a clean and neat appearance. This meant more time spent on washing and ironing. Immigrant women had the added burden, shared with their husbands, of adjusting to the new society. Young women learned some English and could gain some first-hand understanding of American life. Older women often did not learn the new language and, thus, went through life dependent upon others to interpret the language and the culture. For all of these women, native born and immigrant, the club life of the middle-class woman was unknown although ethnic and church organizations did provide occasions for recreation and a means for keeping ethnic identity alive.

■ Childcare

The growth of interest in child development affected the responsibilities of working-class as well as middle-class women. Settlement houses, schools, neighborhood health centers and newspapers stressed the importance of good nutrition, discipline, and regular health examinations. Many programs were devised to insure that the working-class mother, especially the immigrant mother, knew her duty. Some programs, especially those in large cities, also provided means for helping her. In most instances, women were told of their obligations but given little help in meeting them.

Day care was a constant concern of working mothers. In the more fortunate instances a grandmother or other family member was available to care for a pre-school child. After 1895, some older children could spend their after-school time at programs run by settlement houses. Some of the women's organizations provided day-care facilities for children of working mothers but often the requirements of these centers only added to the burdens of an already harassed woman. The Bloomingdale Day Nursery in New York, for example, expected the children of women working 12 hours a day to arrive spotlessly clean at 6:30 in the morning. Children were accommodated only on those days their mothers worked, thus the job-hunting woman or the woman who needed time to attend to other business had to seek an alternative.

■ Education

Education for children in working-class families, although very important, had to be balanced against family economic needs. Whether or not a child, especially a girl, went beyond the legally required primary education depended on the employment opportunities available as well as family needs. By 1900, working-class girls were at least beginning high school. Working-class women, especially the young and the immigrant, were also attending evening classes. They studied English, grammar and spelling, and some earned their high school diploma.

■ Employment

Employment opportunities for working-class women varied with marital status, ethnic or racial background, and education. Unmarried women worked in textile mills and garment factories. When the textile mills first opened in New England in the middle 1800s, they attracted young women from the neighboring towns and countryside. Many of these young women came from families with an independent financial base, a farm, small shop, or other business. The promise of companionship of other young women, the independence offered by dormitory life and the assurance of proper supervision sounded attractive. The reality of life in the mills—long hours, low wages and hard work with little time for companionship—fell far short of its promises. By the end of the century, the mills, like the sweat shops of the garment industry, were the workplace of poor women.

By 1900, young native-born women (white with some high school education) were working alongside their middle-class counterparts as clerks and typists. Poorer women, those less skilled, native born or immigrants, young and old women alike, also worked as servants in the homes of the middle class. A large number of women found employment as laundry workers. Others worked in their own homes doing piece work or laundry. Many women took in boarders to supplement the family income.

For women and men alike working hours were long, 10-hour days, 6 days a week were common, although a 70-hour week was not unusual. Wages, as mentioned, were low: in 1900, women working in garment shops in Boston earned from $3 to $5 per week. In the new department stores, 14- or 15-year-old cash girls probably earned less than $2 per week, and a few years later promotions to sales clerks led to salaries of between $6 and $7 per week. The few cashiers earned from $8 to $10 per week. Women who worked as domestics might earn $1.50 a day if they worked as heavy-cleaning women on a daily basis. Cooks earned the maximum, perhaps $5 a week plus room and board. The pay for women working at home was even lower. Jacob A. Riis reported on women finishing parts for 30 cents a day; others report similar figures.

In her book *We Were There*, Alice Wertheimer, a labor historian, tells the story of working women through 1914. She reports that $800 "was considered the minimum a family of four needed to sustain itself" in an urban area in 1904. Most families were larger, six to eight being the norm. Men's average earnings at that time were $440 per year; women's, $273.

Like their middle-class peers, working-class married women had very limited employment opportunities. The belief that women belonged at home, the assumption that women with children were unreliable workers, and the desire of many employers to staff offices or stores with young, attractive women all mitigated against the married women. Women themselves felt as if there was a stigma attached to their husbands and family if they worked. They responded in different ways. Many women moved in and out of the work force. They worked for pay only when family economic pressures absolutely demanded it. Others, especially those who worked for pay at home, didn't talk about it very much. The wives of shopkeepers, saloonkeepers, and owners of similar service-oriented establishments, like the wives of farmers, "helped out" even though they often worked hours that closely matched their spouses and carried out tasks for which others would have to be paid. Their contribution was indispensable but it did not become part of the economic statistics. (Recently economists have begun to recognize the value of some "helping out" that women do. The statistical category of "unpaid family work" is used to count women and children who work at jobs that require payment if not filled by a family member. Most of the women so counted are agricultural workers in Third World countries.) Because married women could not easily find employment, the situation of widows and women deserted by their husbands, not uncommon, was almost desperate. These women ended up with the jobs unmarried women didn't want—in sweat shops or as servants in very demanding households.

How many women were in the work force at the turn of the century is difficult to determine with accuracy. The assumption that married women did not work was so strong, for example, that census takers did not specifically ask women if they worked for pay until instructed to do so in 1910. Many women, in turn, did not volunteer the fact that they were working to earn money for the family. The census of 1910 records that 19.8 percent of married women worked as opposed to 13.3 percent in 1900. In 1900, it is also worth noting, 41 percent of all non-white women were employed, married or not, while only 17 percent of all white women worked outside the home. It was taken for granted that the bias against working married women did not apply to black women who along with immigrant women, were domestic and laundry workers.

▪ A Humanizing Culture

The culture of the poor and working people from 1890 to 1915 was shaped by some very distinct elements: their own immigrant or rural culture, middle-class attitudes about poverty, and the hope of a better life. Many of these people were immigrants or the children and grandchildren of immigrants. They came to America filled with dreams and strong hope. Even when the conditions of life snuffed these dreams out for them, there remained a hope that things would be better for the next generation. Families, parents and children, were willing to make what today seems unbelievable, sacrifices to educate some of the children, to establish a small business, or bring another member of the family to the United States.

Extended family ties were important. When families were able to settle together, the mutual support they offered each other mitigated some of life's harshness. Grandmothers' cared for young children. There was at least some food during periods of unemployment, as well as support for a widow left without other resources. In addition, there were loved ones with whom to share pleasures and joys, and to enjoy memorable family celebration. Migration and early death—average life expectancy was about 49 years in 1900—left many families without those ties.

American attitudes toward poverty were also part of the popular culture. Two themes twisted together: poverty was good provided one worked hard to overcome it; and poverty was due to a lack of virtue and an inadequate character. Thus, those no longer poor could be proud of their humble beginnings but the existing poor had no one to blame but themselves. The best way to deal with poverty, it was held, was for the middle class by their good example and personal support to raise standards of decency, cleanliness, thrift, and morality among the poor. These attitudes not only affected middle-class response to the poor but influenced the poor themselves. Poverty was not just a burden but a shameful burden. Self-respect demanded that poverty be kept hidden. The onus attached to a working mother was reduced if the income was used for a special good—education of a child or saving for a home or business. Even then, however, women downplayed their jobs for their employment indicated poverty. These attitudes toward poverty were mitigated somewhat in the 1900s as research began to link poverty to low wages, unemployment, sickness, and the ghetto environment.

Finally the harshness of daily life was balanced by the expectation that life would improve. It had for others. Almost everyone knew families that had achieved a better life. And for many, life did improve. Slowly, unevenly, as opportunities expanded and families adjusted to the demands of urban life, income rose, and living conditions improved. Small securities, such as jobs with pensions, some insurance, and education, moved many families, especially white families, into the middle class.

The 1920s

Even as parts of the social agenda of the progressives were being translated into social policy, ideas that were to reshape women's roles once more were emerging. New ideas about marriage and child care, new technologies, advertising, and growing focus on the nuclear family all contributed to redefining women's responsibilities.

The redefinition of women's roles accompanied the emergence of other patterns of ideas and behavior that are still with us. The process by which the United States became a middle-class society was firmly established during the 1920s. The history of that process is beyond the scope of this study. However, before examining the specific change in women's lives, it would be worthwhile to look briefly at three of these wider societal changes: mass production, the growth of advertising and the mass media, and the end to unlimited immigration.

Building a Middle-Class Society

■ Mass Production
Henry Ford introduced the assembly line with a combination of labor-saving processes into his automobile plant in 1912. Within the year he also increased his workers wages an unprecedented $5 a day minimum. The assembly line facilitated the mass production of goods at lower cost; higher wages permitted the worker to buy the goods he or she made. Other manufacturers were slow to adopt Ford's wage policy but they were relatively quick to adopt the assembly line, especially when World War I called for more goods. When the war ended the assembly line was an established manufacturing technique. During the 1920s a range of consumer goods were mass produced and because of their relatively low cost became accessible to many families. More and more families had or expected to soon have the symbols of a middle-class style of life: a car, a radio, household appliances, and even a home.

■ The Media
The mass media and advertising also contributed to the process of building a nation whose people consider themselves middle class. Referring to the *Saturday Evening Post,* Frederich Lewis Allen

in his popular history *The Big Change* points out "that through this five cent magazine, and others like it, millions of Americans were getting a weekly or monthly inoculation in ways of living and of thinking that were middle-class, or classless American . . . . " Magazines complemented the attitudes and values being promoted in the schools where every effort was made to train young people to be good Americans.

The radio played a role in this process by offering rich and poor alike entertainment and a common explanation of the events of the day. Later motion pictures provided a graphic model of the American way of life. Advertisement and media tended to promote a common set of myths about how Americans lived. As their economic conditions allowed, growing numbers of Americans translated the myths into reality.

■ Immigration Policies

Between 1921 and 1924 the United States adopted a series of laws that ended the relatively unrestricted and unlimited immigration policies of the past. The laws were biased against eastern and southern Europeans as well as blacks and Orientals. As a consequence of the laws, the pool of low-skill, low-paid, foreign-born workers was sharply reduced and the real wages of workers began to climb. The ghettos where immigrants first settled began to shrink, until internal migrants, for example, southern blacks, and Hispanics from Puerto Rico and the southwest, began to move to the cities. The end of immigration also ended the development of alternatives to the emerging national culture.

■ The 1920s Set a Pattern

The United States did not become a middle-class nation in the 1920s. Frederick Lewis Allen (*The Big Change*), for example, reports that in 1929 Brookings Institution economists estimated that it cost a family $2000 just for annual basic necessities and about 60 percent of U.S. families had yearly incomes below that level. Rather the practices and attitudes that in fact became the dominant experience after World War II became firmly rooted in our society in the 1920s. Many of those families whose economic and social situations placed them in sharp contrast to the evolving mores expected to share in them in the future, therefore they too subscribed to them. The media tended increasingly to ignore alternative experiences and our myths began to deny their existence.

Women's Roles

Prior to World War II there were some tentative challenges to the commonly accepted notions of marital relations and child care. After the war these concepts became the guides for a new style of life. Earlier a woman's role as wife was considered secondary to that of mother and homemaker. By 1920 women were being urged to reverse these priorities. Psychologists, sociologists, doctors, and publicists were claiming more and more loudly that women could only be truly happy if they devoted themselves to being a good wife to their husbands. In order to be good wives, women were told, they had to be interested in their husbands' activities while making their homes comfortable havens. Colleges became important hunting grounds for husbands as well as places where young women learned the new social graces. Sororities grew in popularity and importance. Off campus, new clubs and some of the old clubs taught women to play bridge and other games. Publicists reached working-class women through magazines and newspapers. Personal appearance, an interesting personality, and friendships were the goals identified for and by young women. The "flapper" became the trend setter of the day.

Five factors were important in bringing this change in focus about: new knowledge about sexuality, a new approach to birth control, changes in the social function of the family, limits on women's participation in decision-making despite their education, and new approaches to childrearing.

■ **Sexuality and Birth Control**

Psychology began to probe sexuality and attributed many of people's problems to repressed sexuality. Even those who did not share the problems learned of the need to give sex a different place in their lives. Women were told the Victorians were wrong, that they could and should enjoy sex.

Margaret Sanger affirmed that women could and would enjoy sex if they controlled the number and spacing of their children. She argued as well that fewer children benefited women and the society as a whole. Prior to 1900 birth control was considered immoral and unacceptable to any respectable woman. In addition, birth control techniques were few: abstinence, the condom, withdrawal, and douches were subject to failure, and in many states the condom was illegal. By 1920, as Alfred Kinsey's sex histories show, urban, educated Protestant women were increasing their efforts at birth control. The introduction of the diaphram in the early 1920s provided women with a birth control device that was convenient and controllable.

Margaret Sanger and other supporters of birth control began a multifaceted campaign to publicize and legalize contraceptives and birth control clinics, which did not become completely successful until 1965. They talked about wanted children, the need for proper care for children families already had, feminine hygiene and health, the importance of sex in marraige and the value of birth control in restricting the growth in numbers of the poor and unfit. Even those women who opposed birth control or those without access to contraceptives, which were often illegal and usually available only to those who could pay, were influenced by the movement. At the very least, women gained an understanding of their bodies. More often, ideas associated with the birth control discussion combined with those of psychologists to change concepts about the purpose and nature of marriage.

■ A New Role for Families

Sociologists were also advocating change in family relationships, without which they feared for the family's survival as an institution. From a sociological perspective the family had been the basic economic producer as well as social unit. Industrialization undermined the family's productive* role. Many observers feared that unless the productive role was replaced the nuclear family especially would not survive, that divorce would become widespread, and that society would be disrupted. From this perspective the stress on personal relationships and service, especially responsibilities of wives to husbands, was a welcomed new focus for the family.

The sociologists concern was valid but whether it had much meaning for the majority of families in the 1920s is another question. For most families, women's contributions to family well-being were economic as well as psychological and social. If women were not in the work force and contributing earnings, their contributions in the form of food preparation, sewing, and similar services were significant. Even so, the sociologists concern was one of more contribution promoting attention to the marital relationship.

■ Educated Women

The college graduates of 1900, the trend-setters of that time, expected that women, once educated, would be given the opportunity to participate significantly in society and business. Despite the importance of women's contributions to the Progres-

---

*The word "productive" is used in this text in a technical sense to indicate that a particular task or activity has economic value whether or not the individual doing it is paid and whether or not its economic value is counted by economists or government statisticians. Thus, for example, a woman who sews for her family is doing productive work. Listening to her children, although of great value, does not have economic value and, therefore, in the sense the word is used in the text, is not productive.

sive Era, women's opportunities were limited. The barriers were such that relatively few women became decision-makers and most areas of decision were confined to the women's sphere: child care, elementary education, nursing, social work, and other areas that related to women. Young women in 1915 or 1925 could look at college alumnae and clearly see the limits of involvement. Women could not vote until 1920. Despite their interest and efforts to improve health, decisions were made by doctors and only 10 percent of all doctors were women. Women accounted for only 2 percent of all lawyers.

Those women who did achieve any measure of success were rarely married. Doctors and psychologists attributed the frustration and unhappiness of older graduates to their choosing the wrong goals in life rather than the employment and social barriers they faced. The experts' response was to urge young women to choose more appropriate goals.

Students, consciously or unconsciously accepting the status quo as unchangeable, tended to follow these experts advice. Women's attendance at both high school and college continued to increase. However, social life on campus became as important as intellectual life. The colleges themselves stressed the former when appealing to women and their parents. The barriers to graduate education remained formidable, thus, women's participation in graduate education did not significantly expand: women earned 30 percent of all master's degrees in 1920 and 33 percent in 1930. Over the course of the decade women's share of Ph.D.'s and equivalent degrees remained the same 15 percent.

■ Childrearing in the 1920s

All these factors would have generated challenges to previous definitions of women's role but probably would not have significantly changed that role as long as women believed in the importance of their role as child nurturers. But beginning in the 1920s that too was brought into question. Child development specialists were now telling women that too much maternal love and attention were stifling and harming children. Women were warned to carefully regulate their children's lives according to firm schedules. Infants needed a regime of feeding, play, and sleep. Unscheduled attention to a crying baby would only spoil the child. Early schooling was good for children because it allowed experts to direct their activities and growth, and freed the child to develop independence and its own interests. Women were to create the environment in which children were to grow. Beyond that, less was best. Doctors, educators, and other child development specialists agreed with other experts that women's first priorities should be their relationship with their husbands and the maintenance of their homes so as to create environments that supported families. Having done this, they should then provide the necessary care to their children.

■ Women and Work

The shifts in women's employment patterns during the 1920s, although not major, reflected society's ideas of what was appropriate. Women's work force participation increased by 1 percent during the decade. As in the past, women's wages were significantly less than those of men, yet Labor Department statistics indicated that about 90 percent of working women were motivated by economic need.

The weight of protective legislation, enacted during the previous decade, was evident as women's share of manual work dropped. Employment expanded for clerical workers and other white-collar workers, teachers, and nurses, for example. Sales opportunities also expanded: about a million new jobs were created during the 1920s, yet women captured only a small share, about 20 percent. Service jobs also increased as the new attention to appearance generated a demand for hairdressers and beauticians. Although men set the trends and became the experts, women filled most of these new jobs.

Women and the Changed Social Environment

■ Appliances

By 1920 running water, bathrooms, and electricity were quite common in the urban home. Electricity and running water opened the way for household appliances. Washing machines, refrigerators, and gas or electric stoves were followed by toasters, vacuum cleaners, and other appliances. Each of these appliances eased the drudgery and time required to maintain a family.

The marketing of prepared food also reduced the time women had to spend in the kitchen. The first prepared foods were canned goods and preserves followed by baked goods. (Sheila Rothman, Women's Proper Place, estimates that as early as 1900 about 90 percent of urban homes used bakers' bread.) The use of these products spread and by the 1920s some commonly prepared food was a staple in every household.

■ The Suburbs

Although the automobile was not a household appliance it too contributed to significant changes in a woman's day. Women could and did travel further to shops and for pleasure. Activities once limited to the few with money or to a rare occasion became more available. The beaches, the mountains, and travel itself became a part of the life of a growing number of families.

More importantly, the automobile opened the possibility of suburban living to more people. With an automobile, wage earners, assumed to be men, could travel to work even if trains or other public transportation were not available. A family could now have its own home with grass and trees away from the crowded city.

Suburban living offered the family, especially the young family, other advantages, not the least of which was separation from parents. In order for the relationship between husband and wife to develop correctly, the growing conventional wisdom asserted, young married people needed privacy and independence from parental and other family ties. The suburbs allowed this. Suburban living not only justified physical distance from other family members, it also reduced the possibility of multigenerational families. Many of the new homes had no room for extra relatives. Only a minority of U.S. families lived in the suburbs—less than 10% in 1930. However, a home in the suburbs began to be defined as the American ideal.

■ Advertising and the Media

The growth in advertising also contributed to women's new environment. Women's magazines were a major outlet for advertisement. In addition to traditional articles on home management, entertainment, and child care, the magazines displayed the consumer goods that American manufacturers were beginning to develop. If these publications did not displace the advice customarily handed from mother to daughter, they at least became an important complement to it.

Advertisements also began to erode the value of some of the homemakers traditional tasks. Appealing descriptions stressing the special advantage of a commercially prepared cake, doll, dress, or sweater caused homemade baked goods, toys, or clothing to seem old-fashioned and inferior. In the 1920s the economics of mass production had not reduced the cost of many manufactured goods below what it would be if made by an efficient homemaker. Thus "homemade" was still common. However, "bought" was becoming a status symbol. And many traditional skills, such as knitting, were not being passed on.

■ A New Situation

In 1880 or even 1900, the young homemaker possessed a substantial array of skills. She could not only cook and keep a home but usually she had experience with caring for children and the eldelry. Many had also taken care of ill family members. Most women, therefore, had at least minimal confidence that they could handle a variety of crises either alone or with the help of an especially competent neighbor or relative. Between 1900 and 1930 not only did experts begin telling women how to care for children but they told them how to manage other aspects of family life. The doctor, for example, looked upon any area of health as his responsibility and set about excluding the non-professional. Well-baby clinics, the domain of public health nurses supported by social workers and volunteers, were challenged by doctors so effectively that by 1930, they were no longer used by any family that could afford a doctor. With the attention to sexuality and birth control, doctors took on the role of sexual counselors. In both cases, health maintenance and sexuality, doctors were not much more informed than the experienced lay person, yet the latter increasingly deferred to the former.

By 1930, many homemakers lacked confidence in their own ability to carry out some of the responsibilities their mother took for granted. They did not feel competent to deal with the ill or with invalids. They looked to experts for guidance in child care. Some even relied on the writer and publicist to tell them how to keep husbands happy and run the household. In effect, professional-ization of some of women's traditional tasks coupled with smaller homes and new family priorities tended to reduce women's sphere of activity. Within 20 years many practices introduced in the 1920s, such as the isolation of the nuclear family and the dominance of commercially prepared food, would be the common experience.

1930 to 1950

The stock market crash of 1929 was followed by the most severe depression in U.S. history. Ten years later recovery was underway but progress was slow. It was not until the United States became involved with World War II, first as the "arsenal for democracy" then as a combatant, that the Depression ended. Unemployment and inflation were a part of the post-war economic adjustment. However, the worst fears were not realized as the GI Bill, the demand for consumer goods, the Cold War and the Korean War all eased the transition to a civilian-oriented economy with fuller employment.

For women this was a time of contrasts, but not a time of evolving theories or new advice. Those who could, continued to live by the theories and myths of the past. Those who had to change viewed their previous way of living as the norm to be returned to when conditions allowed.

During the Depression every effort was made to keep women out of the work force. Women were dismissed from the Civil

Service under a "married person's" clause when a reduction in personnel was necessary. Men received preference in government sponsored jobs. Nevertheless, women found ways to earn; in fact, between 1930 and 1940 about two million additional women entered the work force, raising women's participation rate to 24 percent.

Women once again became active in public life. Many of those in the work force joined labor unions; others became members of the many grassroots organizations designed to protect people and their homes. During the 1937 strikes at the General Motors Company plants in Flint, Michigan, that led to the recognition of the United Auto Workers, for example, women formed the Emergency Brigade. In order to avoid unfavorable publicity, women employees were asked to leave the plants by union organizers when the sitdown strikes began. As the film "Babies and Banners" records, these women and the wives of strikers began operating a soup kitchen but soon moved to the picket line. Placing themselves between strikers and police during clashes they reduced the opportunities for injury and by their courage and outspokenness gained supporters. They prevented company guards from firing tear gas into strikers at a key plant, an event which proved to be a turning point in the strike.

World War II brought a sharp turnabout. Women were welcomed into factories, shops, and just about anywhere they were willing to work. Women became the skilled workers in airplane and converted auto plants. Women drove taxies and took new responsibilities in the government. Each branch of the armed services had its women's component. Women served close to the front lines as nurses and flew transport planes across the country and the world.

Whether in the work force or not, women made decisions about issues they had previously left to their husbands. They retrieved long forgotten homemaking skills and acquired some new ones as they became chief maintenance workers around the house. Although they would not say it in just this way, women showed themselves to be very capable persons.

Women's responsibilities for children and home were acknowledged but minimally acted upon. The Federal Government proposed day care centers for children but even as late as 1945 less than 10 percent of the need was being met. Some child care specialists voiced concern about the well-being of children but offered no alternatives to full-time mothering, which the nation could not afford. When the war ended most women returned home. They were told that their patriotic duty required that they give their jobs to returning soldiers. Their husbands and children needed them at home. Even their own happiness required it. Yet, in

1950, women made up 29.6 percent of the labor force.

From the perspective of ideas about women's roles it was as if the previous 15 years had not happened. The models held out to women and accepted by many were intensified versions of those that dominated the 1920s. Women were first and foremost to make their husbands and children happy by being the perfect companions and homemakers. They were to supply their children with just the right amount of love and support. In return they too would be happy people.

The Past Thirty Years

The 1950s brought strong and substantial economic growth that benefited most sections of society. Employment in every occupational category expanded. The GI Bill assured the availability of the well-educated work force needed for the increased numbers of technical and professional jobs. Suburbs grew rapidly to meet the demand for more housing with the help of major government investment in roads. The dream of owning a home became a possibility for millions because of the GI Bill, lower down payment requirements, and higher wages.

The model held out to women was that of the suburban homemaker but not all women followed that model. In addition, the events of the 1960s challenged many of the values the suburbs cherished. In the midst of all this women continued to seek an education and increasingly became a part of the work force.

Suburban Life Becomes the Model

The homemaker welcomed the suburban life. New, clean housing areas without city congestion made it easier for her to focus on what she was to do—care for her family. Neighbors could provide companionship. The family car and the telephone served to keep her in touch with the rest of the family. New appliances and processed food cut down on some of the demands of the housework and raised others. Since spotless cleanliness became an achievable idea, it seemed as though only laziness explained a less than perfectly clean and ordered home.

The family became a renewed focus of expert and popular attention. In the process the family came to be defined as the nuclear family. Magazines, T.V., and film first portrayed the family as parents and four children. By 1970, family size had dropped to two children. Sociologists, economists, and other professionals were working from the same perspective. This shift was understandable because for many families the extended family was not a functioning reality.

The war time experiences of travel and living in different regions of the country encouraged many young people to settle away from the areas in which they had grown up. Employment opportunities and demands moved extended families further apart. Upward mobility in a corporation might mean 15 moves in 20 years. Technical and skilled workers also moved to obtain better paying jobs. Where a family finally set down roots depended on a set of circumstances the least important of which was the location of the rest of the family.

House designs and child psychology reinforced the retreat to the nuclear family. There was no room for an extra member of a family in many suburban tract houses or in city apartments. Child development experts and doctors talked of the importance of each child having a room of her/his own. In time it became acceptable to admit that caring for an elderly family member was often a burden. With people living longer, usually in adequate health, older people, younger families, and the community began devising alternatives to an elderly parent living with a grown child and her or his family.

The model of the nuclear family living in suburbia, however, held many contradictions, especially for women. As we examine women's experiences it is important to keep in mind that, as in the past, women evaluated their experiernces in quite different ways. Many women have managed the contradictions successfully and happily. The problems and difficulties, although very real, have been more than compensated for by the many rewards suburban family life offered. For some others the rewards have not balanced the costs. The majority of women probably fall into a third category. While not condemning suburban life they clearly recognized its limits and often acted to change it.

■ Women in Suburbia

In addition to the traditional-living imposed responsibilities of food preparation, family and home maintenance, homemakers found that suburban living imposed some new chores. As mentioned earlier, the standards for housekeeping became greater as the availability of appliances and new products enabled women to get things cleaner and neater. Because of these different standards, many appliances sold as time/work savers in fact increased women's work. Women with babies and small children faced days just about as demanding as those lived by women in earlier times. This was especially true if they had two or more pre-school age children. There was no one to help out. Domestic help was usually not available; relatives who might have lent a hand in the past were not present. Neighbors were usually in the same overworked situation. In this instance, one of the touted attractions of the suburbs, being with similar families, was a disadvantage. The one source of help available to some women was the teenage girl who took children out for an hour or two after school. The same babysitter became vital to the family's social life: her availability had to be established before any plans could be made (some teenage boys also found babysitting a good source of spending money).

The lack of public transportation made chauffeuring a major chore for women. In one-car families, women often began the day by driving husbands to the train or bus station. If children were to partake in organized recreation or visit with friends, mothers had to get them there and back. Shopping, doctor's visits, just about any errand, required a drive. The end of the neighborhood store that accompanied the growth of shopping centers also increased women's driving—a child could no longer be sent to buy milk or bread.

Privacy became isolation. When the novelty of the life style wore off, many women found themselves lonely and housebound. Neighbors became friends but different daily schedules and frequent moves often prevented the sharing that promotes deep friendships. And at six o'clock, when the men returned, the neighborhood hustle and bustle ended, as couples sought to build their family and their own relationships.

The organization of suburban living around family, family being defined as parents and children, segregated women according to a variety of factors. The long-standing divisions based on race and class continued. Until the mid-1960s, few blacks were found in the suburbs; almost all of those lived in clearly recognized black areas. The cost of housing and taxes created class distinctions among areas. In addition, suburban living encouraged separations based on age and marital status. When children had grown many families found suburban homes too large. Retirees often judged their homes too expensive or too demanding of their energy. Furthermore, the majority of social activities, whether sponsored by church, civic association, or club, were geared to the interests of families or younger couples. Older people often felt they didn't belong. In many suburbs, there were relatively few people over 60 and sometimes couples in their 50s were rare. With the exception of those with children, single people also felt they did not belong in the suburbs.

This segregation impoverished the lives of suburban women and their children as well. Most women met and interacted with women of very similar circumstances. They had very little opportunity to learn first-hand about experiences of older or poorer people, or people of different racial backgrounds, or of the new immigrants. The isolation from the experiences of people in different situations left suburban women puzzled and disturbed by the disruptions of the sixties. Because of their work contacts, men were usually a little better prepared to deal with the forces of change.

Women expected that the love and togetherness of a marriage would provide all the satisfactions they would need. This was not realized. Husbands, tired and under stress from work situations, often wanted only care and comfort. They could not and did not meet either the emotional or intellectual needs of their wives. Marital tensions piled on top of the weariness and frustrations for both spouses and undermined the core of women's lives. The rise in the divorce rate was an important indicator of this dissatisfaction.

■ Renewed Interest in Education

As women moved to the suburbs, so too they moved to higher education.

Thirty-six percent of all college graduates were women in 1955. Ten years later as part of the general expansion in college attendance well over twice as many women graduated and they accounted for 40 percent of the degrees awarded. These figures do not tell the full story, for many more women attended college than graduated. Increasing numbers of women began to seek graduate education. Slowly, from a low of 9 percent in 1955, women began to claim a larger portion of Ph.D.'s and other professional degrees; by 1978 women's share had risen to 26 percent.

Not only have a significant number of women gone on to college in the past 25 years, they have also chosen to study an even wider range of subjects. Women enrolled in accounting, engineering, and agriculture as well as literature, history, and the social sciences. The march on professional schools began in earnest in the late 1960s. In 1973, for example, there were three and one-half times as many women in law school as in 1969. In the same period the number of women attending medical school almost doubled.

Education influenced women's lives in different ways. The majority of women prior to the mid-1960s expected that they would use their education primarily as wives and mothers. A part of that expectation was the assumption that they would find intellectual stimulation in that setting. For many this assumption was not realized. The frustrations that resulted contributed to women's dissatisfactions with suburban living. Some women found the intellectual outlets they sought in volunteer work; others found or created part-time or full-time work outside the home. A substantial number of educated suburban women were ready to respond when the women's movement called for a change.

Other Models

To most black women, the models of suburban life held before them by the mass media and society's mainstream were alien. Economic necessity required many of these women to be part of the work force even if married and with young children. Racism not only restricted them and their husbands to low-paying jobs but dictated where they could live, and what community services were available to them. The heritage of slavery and the pattern of response to current social stress left many women with sole responsibility for themselves and their children. The extended family still served an important function; grandmother, aunts, and sisters-in-law often shared child care and other tasks. It was not uncommon for a child to spend extended periods of time with an aunt or grandmother.

The frustrations of the black community exploded into action in December 1955 when Rosa Parks, a middle-aged seamstress, refused to move from her seat on a Montgomery, Alabama, bus. Mrs. Parks, returning home from work, was arrested. The resulting boycott of public transportation was finally ended when the federal courts ordered the integration of public transportation. The civil rights movement, which grew out of Rosa Park's stand, changed the economic and social situation of many black women and served as a model for the later women's movement.

Women in white ethnic families, particularly those of Italian and Eastern European heritage, also experienced the 1950s and 1960s differently from many other Americans. For one thing, a larger portion of these women and their families stayed in the cities and inner suburbs. Fewer went on to higher education. Their families did not reap quite as many economic benefits as those in the mainstream in part because male workers tended to be skilled workers rather than managers or technicians. For these women, as for black women, the extended family was a strong viable force in their lives. Moreover, homemaking retained its status among ethnic women despite its losses elsewhere. This reflects the reality of ethnic women's lives. They have always been a part of the work force—family economics have required it. They have usually had hard, boring, and low-paying jobs. In contrast, homemaking has been a freeing, self-directed activity with economic and social value.

For a third group of women the recent past has been a time of testing new experiences. There have always been single women in our society but since the 1950s their ranks have grown and changed in composition. Once, most single women were young women waiting for marriage or widows. Today there are more single women and they are found in every age bracket. Divorce has been an important contributing factor but it alone does not account for the increased number of single women. Since 1960, many women have decided to postpone marriage and others have decided not to marry. Census statistics show that in 1978 almost half the young women between 20 and 24 had not married, a two-thirds increase in unmarried women compared with 1960.

Many factors contribute to the decision to postpone or eschew marriage. The rate of marriage failure has to be one. However, economic factors are probably a major consideration. It is possible today for a woman alone to be self-sufficient. She can earn enough to provide herself with decent housing, adequate food, and enough money to meet other expenses. In the past, employment opportunities and housing were much more limited.

As in the past, women with children must struggle to manage money and time. Even so, it is usually easier for these women than it was 20 years ago. Despite their increased numbers and self-sufficiency, single women are often not fully accepted. They are at one and the same time pitied for their failure to catch or hold a man and questioned, even condemned, for wrong priorities.

In building happy, whole lives, single women have challenged some myths about women and have also highlighted some basic human needs. Single women demonstrated that the role of wife and mother is not the only satisfying role for women. They have shown that women can be self-reliant and effective decision-makers. Because they are alone, single women have an immediate appreciation of the importance of friendships and support structures. The latter is especially important although hard to describe and create. The structures that support married women are often not available to single women—they have no husband, for example; parents, brothers, and sisters are sometimes more concerned about finding a husband for a woman than in supporting her in her existing situation. She may not know her neighbors. Yet if a single woman is to be a happy and whole person she, like everyone else, must have contact with persons who listen, encourage, challenge, and respond to her needs. In the business of family life, these basic needs are not always recognized. They become clear in the life of a single person. Recently, because of the sharing encouraged by the women's movement, married women and couples have also come to a better understanding of the value of a support system.

The Challenges of the Sixties

The civil rights movement, the Viet Nam conflict, more effective methods of birth control, and a shifting economy, as well as the women's movement have touched women's lives in some very dramatic ways. (The women's movement will be examined more fully in Chapter 2.)

■ The Civil Rights Movement

The civil rights movement began in the 1950s and grew in momentum until the mid-1960s brought significant changes to the lives of many black people, women and men alike. The movement enhanced the self-respect of black women, imparted a variety of new understandings about our society and skills for effective action in it, and created new economic opportunities. In addition, the movement raised some difficult questions about the relationships between women and men in a racist and sexist society. Since, for example, black women could often find employment when black men could not, should the demands of the movement be structured to enhance the economic opportunities of black men, or should they be sexually neutral? There have been no easy answers to these and similar questions.

The movement influenced white women, especially younger women. Motivated by a sense of justice, many became involved. Their experiences led to a growing consciousness of their own oppressions, and that provided them with a model for action. The women's movement followed.

■ The Viet Nam Conflict

The Viet Nam conflict had multiple effects on women. The counter-culture that evolved as young people questioned the war and the society that sanctioned it challenged conventional thinking. Marriage, family structures, work, and the nature and structure of our society became subject to questioning and experimentation. Many of the values that women were supposed to protect, such as cleanliness, were openly discarded. Ideas and practices first labeled unthinkable and immoral became a part of the common culture a few years later when young "radicals" combined their preferred life style with the need and desire to be wage earners. Women then found the larger society questioning the values and practices that they had been taught to depend upon and defend. For many women this has been a disturbing experience. The Viet Nam conflict also created a group of self-sufficient women. Military wives, once more left on their own, had to cope with the ordinary problems of growing families in extraordinary times. The opposition to the war touched these families in a special way, generating feelings of isolation and alienation. Yet most of the women made the necessary decisions, and gained a new idea about their own judgments and abilities. The climate created by the rising women's movement made it difficult if not imposible for these women to return to traditional roles when their husbands returned. Instead, they, like many other women, wrestled with creating new patterns of sharing responsibility within marriage.

Women took an active part of the anti-war movement itself. As in the case of the civil rights effort, their awareness of their own oppressions grew, they learned of an effective method for bringing about change, and they acquired the skills with which to do so. Thus, the anti-war movement like the civil rights movement, led women into the growing women's movement.

■ New Methods of Birth Control

The civil rights movement and the Viet Nam conflict disrupted society and the lives of women in loud, public ways. The development of new technologies for birth control led to a quieter but more profound change. With the birth control pill, women could regulate fertility in a convenient and highly effective way at relatively little cost. Married women, usually in dialogue with husbands, could and did make decisions about the number and spacing of their children. Plans they made about other aspects of their lives could be made without fear of an unexpected pregnancy. Women argued, for example, that employers were no longer justified in denying women promotions and greater responsibilities on the grounds that they, women, would get pregnant and leave.

The availability of effective low-cost means of birth control coupled with the 1965 Supreme Court decision to legalize abortion set the stage for a new climate of sexuality with positive and negative aspects. Then talk about sexuality and sex encouraged some to adopt more wholesome, human attitudes and others to change values that were immature and exploitive. Women became more knowledgeable about their own sexuality and physiology. In addition to accepting and rejoicing in their sexuality, women have also used their new knowledge to make demands on the medical establishment for better reproductive and general health care. On the negative side, young people, especially young women, find themselves under pressure to be sexually active even when not ready to deal responsibly with all that is involved.

Sexuality and reproduction have been the most contentious of the issues raised during the 1960s. In a special way these issues touch our personal and communal lives. Because public policy is involved, discussion of sexuality and reproduction has moved into the public arena. As a consequence, the issues have been argued in very narrow terms, often labeled pro life or pro abortion. Recently, women and men who see the issues as more involved, who recognize that decisions about abortion, for example, involve many elements, not just personal preference, are raising new questions in the debate. Whether or not society can frame a complex of laws that protect life for infants and women is yet to be seen.

Women in the Work Force: Response to a Shifting Economy

Labor Department statistics show that in 1979 over 43 million women, half of all women 16 and older, were in the labor force. Many but not all of the women who had responded to the need for more workers during World War II did return home after 1945. However, women's rate of participation in the work force did not fall back to pre-war levels and as early as 1955 slowly began to increase. Women about 40 or older accounted for most of this growth until 1965, when they were joined by women between the ages of 24 and 35.

This change in the participation of women in the work force has had consequences for every aspect of our society, thus analysts have sought explanations. There is no one answer. New job opportunities, changes in the economy, the women's movement, and education have all influenced women's decision to work outside the home.

The Viet Nam conflict began in the midst of an expanding economy and added to the already increased need for more clerical and other white-collar workers. Employers actively sought women to meet the need. But, even as some women were being drawn into the work force by the availability of jobs, others were being forced into the job market by the loss of jobs.

The movement of manufacturing plants begun after World War II has accelerated in recent years. Some manufacturers such as textile manufacturers have moved their operations from the industrialized north to the south and southwest in order to take advantage of the lower wages of a non-unionized work force. Transnational corporations seeking increased profits and access to global markets have been shifting production facilities to Asia, Latin America, and the Caribbean. U.S. transnationals and foreign firms have increased their imports of goods ranging from shoes to T.V. sets to auto parts into the United States. Other firms, also seeking to decrease costs and increase profits, have begun automating some processes. Factory jobs have disappeared, and alternatives have not kept up with the need. Unemployment has climbed. This process has been accompanied by high inflation rates that have been highest for basic necessities: food, housing, hospital care, and transportation. Education costs rose. Families have discovered that they needed more than one income to manage so more women joined the work force.

The women's movement helped legitimize middle-class women's decisions to work outside the home. The movement provided women with the opportunity to voice their complaints about homemaking and advertised the advantages of a job or career.

Education also influenced women's decision about work outside the home. Women, like men, had been making educational choices with an eye to future employment. Finishing their education they sought to put it and themselves to the test of a job. Those women who studied in fields once restricted to men, business and science, for example, were especially anxious to build a career. Economic circumstances and anti-discrimination laws created the needed opportunities.

Often the attention given to working women had focused on women entering non-traditional jobs, carpentry, telephone repair, or space engineering, but most women have found employment in jobs that have been traditionally women's. Eighty percent of the female work force are found in clerical, sales, women's factory, or service jobs. When men and women hold the same job, pay is equal; however, most women's work is titled differently from men's and the pay is not equal. Women average 50 percent of what men earn and the gap continues to widen.

Within the last few years, women determined to change their working conditions have organized in increasing numbers. Women have always been part of the labor movement. However, recent organizing efforts have reached beyond past attempts. Trade union women, responding to the need to focus the unions' attention on concerns of women, formed the Coalition of Labor Union Women in 1974. About the same time women office workers in Chicago, Boston, San Francisco, and Cleveland began to organize. Using publicity and education, these groups have mobilized women and forced businesses to change practices that locked women into low-skill, low-paying jobs.

The presence of women in large numbers in the work force has challenged much past thinking and promises to raise more questions. Flexible working hours, shared time, and equal pay for work of equal value, questions raised by women, will be, along with plant movings, spreading automation and the role of labor unions and economic questions before us in the 1980s.

Over the past hundred years the roles of women have changed yet much remains the same. Motherhood and homemaking have remained the core of women's responsibilities. In the pre-industrial past that core was complemented by a productive responsibility that incorporated women into the society and enhanced their status. With industrialization, women's opportunities for economic contributions were sharply reduced. Professionalization reduced many of her nurturing and caring responsibilities. Most women found themselves confined to home, responsible for creating a human, loving environment for husband and children within a society that placed great value on competition, efficiency, and assertiveness. They were cut off from the intellectual life of the community and with access to the decision-making process that shaped the society.

Recently women have begun to claim a place in public life. In the effort they have challenged many assumptions about women's nature and the structure of society. Whether or not we can create a society that allows women a role in public life, provide them with a fair share of societal benefits and yet strengthen our basic human institutions is yet to be determined.

The following chapters explore some of the issues that must be resolved before we have an answer.

Suggested Readings

Elise Boulding, *The Underside of History: A View of Women Through Time* (Westview Press, Boulder, Colorado, 1976). An overview of the history of women which focuses to the extent permitted by our knowledge on the experiences of ordinary women.

Ellen Goodman, *Turning Points.* (Doubleday, New York, 1979)
The stories of women and men whose lives have been influenced by the women's movement in the United States.

Sheila M. Rothman, *Woman's Proper Place* (Basic Books, Inc., New York, 1979).
A study of the changing ideas about U.S. women's roles from 1870 to the present with an emphasis on the period prior to 1930.

Barbara Mayer Wertheimer, *We Were There: The Story of Working Women in America* (Pantheon Books, New York, 1977).
A history of working women in the United States to World War I.

2.
THE WOMEN'S MOVEMENT

The women's movement that burst upon our society in the early 1970s is the second phase of the effort by U.S. women to share fully in all aspects of our nation's life. Its roots lie in the values of justice and freedom that as a nation we are proud of and in the struggles of women through history for survival and dignity.

A History to Build Upon

Women's movements have grown out of women's time-honored practice of coming together for support and aid. Sometimes movements have sprung up to meet women's specific need. Elise Boulding, in her comprehensive study, *The Underside of History*, tells of women from the city and countryside gathering in Rome in 195 BC to press for the repeal of a law restricting what women could own and how they could travel. The law was repealed and women gained the right to own gold and ride in horse drawn carriages. At other times women have acted for the society. The Book of Exodus tells us of the time when Pharoah ordered that all newborn Jewish boys be killed at birth. Midwives and mothers acted together to frustrate Pharaoh's order, and infants survived.

Usually women's movements have aimed at benefiting both women and the larger society; the Beguine Movement of the Middle Ages is one such example. That movement created opportunities for women to exercise control over their own lives while helping women and children survive and maintaining schools and hospitals. Beguines provided shelter and work for the women and children displaced by the social upheavals of 13th- and 14th-Century Europe. The women formed self-directed religious communities and after a period of conflict won recognition as secular communities from the religious authorities whose sanctions they needed if they were to continue. The Beguine Movement illustrates two characteristics common to women's movements: 1) the style of the movement reflects the values of the society; Beguinism was a religious movement in a time when religion dominated every aspect of life; and 2) women's movements occur when the major structures of a society are changing; 13th- and 14th-Century Europe was industrializing and urbanizing.

Although a few women gained some prominence during the Renaissance, the situation of women remained somewhere between desperate and unenviable during much of Western history. Usually the lives of men were not much better, except that men could take some control over their own lives; women were controlled first by their fathers, later by their husbands.

The second half of the 18th Century was a time of new ideas about the relationships among persons. Equality and liberty were common ideas. Men easily claimed these rights, but women, too, on both sides of the Atlantic, were influenced. Abigail Adams, in a now famous letter to her husband John in March of 1776 asked him to " . . . Remember the Ladies, and be more generous and favorable to them than your ancestors." Less than 20 years later in 1790, Mary Wallstonecraft, an English woman, published *A Vindication of the Rights of Women,* a book that still remains one of the basic documents on women's rights.

Despite the intellectual discussions about the rights of women and the support in terms of funding, service, and even lives that American women contributed to struggle for independence, their rights were not protected in the new nation. The states adopted, as the basis for family codes, English Common Law, which defined husband and wife as one person and that person was the husband. A woman's property, earnings, rights to make decisions, and any other rights she might have were all her husband's once she married. In theory unmarried women had a right to property earnings, and so forth, but in practice these rights were meaningless for all but a few. Even the women who believed that women should control their life and property acted as if they did not for fear of public criticism.

Women's struggle to gain their rights did not begin until 50 years after Abigail Adams' letter to John, and it has progressed unevenly since then. This chapter will briefly review the first phase of that effort, 1826 to 1920, and examine in more detail phase two, from 1960 until the present. In looking at today's women's movement attention will be given to the issues involved and the attitudes and ideas associated with different components of the movement.

Phase One:
Securing Basic Rights

The 19th Century was a time of growth and transformation for the United States. For women it was the time of gaining resources and rights so they might have a voice in shaping their own lives and the nation.

Education

The first phase of the U.S. women's movement began not with struggle, for which it became best known, the fight for women's right to vote, but rather with a push for better education for girls and young women. The arguments put forward by Frances Wright, a Scotish-born writer, traveler, and advocate of women's education, in 1829 as she urged better, more comprehensive education for girls sound very familiar, especially to those concerned about how women are being structured into the process of economic development.

> Until women assume the place in society which good sense and good feeling alike assign to them, human improvement must advance but feebly. It is in vain that we would circumscribe the power of one half of our race, and that half by far the most important and influential. If they exert it not for good, they will for evil; if they advance not knowledge, they will perpetuate ignorance. Let women stand when they may in the scale of improvement, their position decides that of the race. (Quoted from Frances Wright, *Course of Popular Lectures*, 1829.)

Women who sought to improve the educational opportunities for young women knew well the legal and social barriers they faced. Mary Lyon, who founded Mt. Holyoke Seminary in 1837 for example, stayed in another room when the school's male board of trustees talked with potential donors for fear she would offend their sensibilities and lose needed support.

Even when the effort partially succeeded and women were admitted to some colleges, such as Oberlin of Ohio in 1834, there were restrictions on the courses they could take and no effort made to integrate them into the college community. It was not until Vassar opened in 1865 that women were fully accepted into college and offered the same educational opportunities as young men.

Legal Reform

During this same period women were working together to change laws that denied women control of their own earnings and property and practically dispossessed the widows and children of men who died without wills. The issue of control over earnings was particularly compelling because without control over their own earnings, wives of irresponsible men could not even help themselves. The pain and suffering of such women motivated women in state after state to press for changes in the law. In the end, however, it was not women's interests alone that motivated state legislators in the 1840s and 1850s to rewrite women's property rights legislation. Conservative and aristocratic men concerned about safeguarding the fortune of their daughters and wives joined women in urging changes in the law.

Unionizing Efforts

Economic need and changes in the structure of the economy forced women into the work force. Many took piece work home, others worked 12 or more hours in mills or foundries. Pay was always about half that of men, even for the same work. As far back as the 1830s women began organizing to demand better pay and working conditions. As the labor movement grew after the Civil War, women, often with more disdain than support from their male colleagues, contributed substantially to the effort. As in other instances where women struggled for rights, women workers became staunch supporters of suffrage efforts. They saw the vote not as an end in itself but as a means for achieving much needed changes in their work situation.

The Abolition Movement

While some women were arguing for better education for women and others a change in women's legal status, another group was working to end slavery. This effort, like the civil rights movement more than 100 years later, sensitized women to the injustice they faced.

The Grimke sisters were condemned by many, including Massachusetts churchmen, for speaking against slavery at public meetings. In response they included an argument for women's rights in their lectures. When other women were chastised for speaking in public they too began talking of women's rights.

The Seneca Falls Convention of 1848, the First Women's Rights Convention in the United States, was partly the result of the treatment Elizabeth Cady Stanton and Lucretia Mott received at a World Anti-Slavery Convention held in London in 1840. Forced to watch from the gallery because the convention ruled that only men could sit as delegates, these two women began a friendship that led to a lifetime of cooperation and support.

Until the end of the Civil War, the abolitionist and women's rights movements were intertwined. Lucy Stone and Susan B. Anthony, two of the better known suffragists, were agents of the American Anti-Slavery Society. Ellen Carol Du Bois (in *Feminism and Suffrage*) points out that "abolitionism provided the women's rights movement with a theory and practice of social change, a strategy that gave direction to its efforts for female emancipation. The core of . . . [the] strategy was the belief that a revolution in people's ideas must precede and underlie institutional and legal reform in order to effect true social change." The abolitionists saw their demand for an end to slavery as both a demand for change and an education effort aimed at changing public opinion. The suffragists recognized that their cause, too, required public education to backup any legal changes that occurred.

Suffrage

At the First Women's Rights Convention, held in 1848 at Seneca Falls, New York, Elizabeth Cady Stanton offered a resolution on women's suffrage. "Resolved, that it is the sacred duty of the women of this country to secure to themselves their sacred right to elective franchise." It was the only resolution that did not receive unanimous approval. Some present feared that this resolution, quite radical at the time, would discredit women's efforts for more needed changes. Yet, three years later, when Susan B. Anthony canvassed New York State with a petition for the state legislature, the vote was one of the items listed. Still it was not until after the Civil War, and black men but not women secured the right to vote that suffrage became the prime focus of the women's movement.

We can learn much from looking at the suffrage movement. In time it came to appeal to women from almost every segment of society, including a small portion of black and immigrant women. Before that happened, however, before the Tennessee House of Representatives voted in favor of the 19th Amendment in August, 1920, thus securing its ratification, the movement was torn by bitter rivalries, and seemed almost to die.

The Question—How to Win

Strategy and tactics, issues common to today's women's move-ment, divided this earlier effort in 1869 and again in 1914. In 1869, proponents of women's rights split over long-term strategy; in 1914 the issue was tactics.

The late 1860s were a critical time for the women's rights movement. The 14th Amendment, which granted voting rights to all male citizens, was well on the way to being ratified and the 15th Amendment, which made those voting rights specific to blacks, was gaining congressional support. When the women who had worked for the rights of both blacks and women objected, they were urged to be still: it was the black man's time. Disappointed by legislators and their supporters, men and some women alike, women's suffrage advocates formed the National Women Suffrage Association (NWSA) and the American Women Suffrage Association (AWSA) in 1869.

The two organizations represent two answers to an issue that faces every social change oriented organization: does the organization work on a spectrum of related issues or does it focus all its energies on one. Those who established the NWSA, including Elizabeth Cady Stanton and Susan B. Anthony, who had been present at Seneca Falls, chose to link suffrage to other issues of concern to women with the expectation of building support for suffrage over time. The AWSA, growing out of a New England-based organization and supported by such well-known abolition and suffrage advocates as Lucy Stone and her sister Antoinette Brown Blackwell, focused its energies solely on the issue of suffrage and worked at the state rather than the national level. Neither organization could point to any dramatic gains over the next 20 years although both continued to build grassroots support for women's right to vote.

The two organizations united to form the National American Women's Suffrage Association in 1890 and within the decade women secured the right to vote in local elections in Wyoming, Utah, Colorado, and Idaho. By 1911, when a voting rights referendum passed in California, the growth of local groups had revitalized the organization and the movement. However, energies were still focused on the states. In 1912, Alice Paul and Lucy Burns joined the National Association's Congressional Committee with the hopes of reviving the effort for a constitutional amendment. These two women had shared the experiences of English suffragists and began employing marches, demonstrations, and civil disobedience in the effort. These tactics were common in Britain but new to the American movement. Within two years the movement was split again. Unlike 1869, however, the split, bitter as it was, was not followed by a loss of momentum: on June 4, 1919, the Congress passed the women's voting rights amendment on to the states for ratification.

Success and Demise

When the vote was won in 1920, the first phase of the women's movement dissipated. The National Women's Party survived but the other groups faded. Why? Historians and analysts cite many reasons.

Many women expected that once the amendment passed, their work was done: women would have access to any institution, political, civil, or business, they might wish. This expectation was fostered, in part, by the last years of the suffrage movement. In the final push for the vote, many important issues were brushed aside. The final effort did not facilitate the exchange of experience and ideas that had nourished and unified earlier efforts. Women, although working for a common cause, remained in isolated cells. Better educated, middle-class women were ignorant of or unconcerned about the problems of working and poorer women. The argument that women voters, envisioned as white, middle-class women, would help define the nation's values against the immigrants alienated immigrant women and their American born daughters and granddaughters. Black women, courted for a time in the 19th Century, were ignored. The concerns pushed aside prior to World War I were lost to the next generation of women. These women, as pointed out in Chapter I, were turning their attention to their private, domestic lives.

Today's Women's Movement: Phase Two—In Progress

The first signs of a new phase of the movement for women's rights emerged during the tumult of the 1960s. It was not until the early 1970s that the movement captured much public attention. By then it had a strong base.

In the late 1950s a suburban housewife and writer, Betty Friedan, began talking and listening with neighbors and friends. The college-educated homemakers she met complained of feeling empty, dissatisfied, even though they had good husbands, active, happy children, and nice homes. Ms. Friedan began examining and writing about the "problem that had no name." In 1963 *The Feminine Mystique,* questioning traditional concepts about women's happiness, and abilities, became a best seller. The response to this book fed the renewed women's movement.

Roots of Today's Movement

Liberation

Young women were also questioning homemakers' experiences,

their mothers' lives, and a number were looking for alternatives. Some found a meaningful outlet for their concerns for fairness and their skills in the civil rights movement. Long before the movement had achieved its important gains, women were transferring the questions and insights of the civil rights effort to the situation of women. When these women began writing and publishing the ideas they had developed, they provided another resource for questioning women.

The anti-war and related student movements of the 1960s also generated a group of very sensitive women. Their commitment to creating a new society conflicted with the support roles often assigned to them by male leaders. When they found their ideas and resolutions ignored or ridiculed at meetings, women began meeting separately. At first these meetings were mainly sharing and study sessions aimed at exploring the situation of women, though, in time, they led to the formation of strategies for change.

The stream of the women's movement that grew out of the civil rights and student movements, the liberation stream, was largely unorganized and influenced to some degree by the socialist ideal of economic as well as political equality. It was marked as well by a vigorous effort to find alternatives to the hierarchical structures that shaped most organizations. Those involved looked to women's experience, feelings, and insights as guides for what deserved attention. Some, blaming men for their pains and dependency, became violently anti-male. More believed that in order to understand and appreciate women, women's gifts, and themselves as women, they needed to temporarily separate themselves from men and pay more attention to women's experiences and ideas. Most, it almost goes without saying, disagreed with both positions.

Questions of priorities, strategies, what is and is not a woman's issue, and the importance of a socialist perspective were just some of the issues that kept this stream of the movement from forming a national organization. Its philosophy of grassroots autonomy was an equally important factor, as was the involvement of women from different backgrounds. Education and middle-classness were shared, but did not offset differences of income, experience, religion and ethnic background.

NOW: A Focus on Rights

Another stream of the women's movement grew out of the experiences of women in the work force, especially college-educated, professional women. Popular beliefs to the contrary, there were a substantial number of women in the work force and they faced discrimination in the form of low wages and lack of promotion. When in an effort to defeat the Civil Rights Act of 1964, the word sex was added by Rep. Howard W. Smith of Virginia in order to make that part of the act prohibiting discrimination in employment look farcical, women rallied to keep the "joke" in place. The failure of law enforcing agenices to end discriminatory practices was probably the primary prod for the creation of the National Organization of Women (NOW) in 1966.

The women who formed NOW were older and more work-experienced than those who became involved with women's issues through the civil rights and student movements. They expected to use existing legislation, new legislation, and the courts to improve the status of women. They were busy with their own careers and families, however, and, in the early years, did not have much time or inclination to devote energy to organization building. Yet the organization grew; in part because many of its members understood and took advantage of the media, in part because the organization responded to a need of many women despite its disorganization.

NOW's history has been marked by the differences and disagreements that one would expect in a new, national grassroots organization. The Women's Equity Action League (WEAL) is one break-off group. Unconfortable with some of the causes with which NOW had become involved in in 1968, including the Equal Rights Amendment (ERA) and abortion rights, WEAL members chose to focus on legal and clearly economic issues. The NOW Legal Defense and Education Fund was formed largely, it seems, because some members were impatient with NOW's disorganization. Most radical women did not like NOW's structure, its seeming elitism, and its conservatism. Still women continued to join the organization, including women from the liberation stream. NOW became the focus of struggles over issues to be supported, priorities, and the manner in which power was to be distributed between local chapters and a national office. In the process, NOW grew and became more representative.

A Hidden Movement:
Women Religious' Quest for Personhood

Two of the women on NOW's first board of directors were nuns: both Sisters Mary Austin Doherty and Sister Mary Joel Read were educators and School Sisters of St. Francis. Their presence was one sign of a major transformation taking place within women's religious orders. The process began simply enough in the mid-1950s.

Most women religious were teaching and most at that time were beginning their work teaching without teacher certification; a matter of increasing concern for those who were responsible for the sisters and those they taught. After a study in 1956 by Sr. Mary Emil Penet, IHM, the Sisters' Formation Conference was formed and a basic curriculum developed. This new course of study was designed to prepare well-educated, personally developed professionals, with good theological and spiritual backgrounds, and some concern for justice. Not all religious orders followed the new curriculum; however, the commitment to education was just about universal. Because nursing sisters were usually professionally educated before beginning to work, the curriculum had its greatest impact on those who were to become teachers.

To the surprise of those spearheading this movement, their efforts encountered strong opposition from parish pastors and bishops who wanted the women in the classrooms. Since the sisters were not asking for money to finance the increased education but only time, they had not expected any problems. As it was, they had to fight pastors and bishops, the men from whom they expected leadership and support, to achieve their goals.

Since Catholic theological institutes and seminaries severely restricted attendance prior to the mid-1960s, women seeking either an M.A. or Ph.D. in theology or biblical studies attended the special program at St. Mary's of the Woods College, Notre Dame, or earned a degree at a Protestant seminary or secular university (in 1967 the St. Mary's program was ended because those administering it felt that there was no longer a need for it). Increased education led to increased competence and self-confidence. Education in Protestant schools of theology opened a new world of ideas and practices to women who had previously lived isolated from the larger community.

Vatican Council II and the directive that called for the renewal of religious communities through an examination of their founders' and founderesses' life and goals also had profound influences on women religious. The Council called on each order to hold a chapter of renewal within three years and to consult every member of the community. The orders were free to change and experiment with new rules for 12 years. Because of her vow of obedience, every member had to respond—and did. Women spoke out about their feelings and dreams and in time assumed authority to act for renewal. Transformation, in this case, began at the bottom.

The renewal of religious life was not without pain and struggle. The process of change affected individual women and orders in different ways. The majority of women religious struggled with the task of responding to the Vatican II directives while at the same time reflecting the diversity of views within the order and did renew their order. Some women, examining their own lives in light of a new found maturity that grew out of the renewal process, decided that their vocation required something else of them; they left their communities. Others found their lives robbed of meaning, and they too left their communities. Some resisted any change while still others pushed for changes that went far beyond what many religious, as well as the rest of the church, were willing to accept. For the women who remained in religious life, the period of rapid change seems to have ended and it is now time to test the new rules by living with them.

The process of change did much to increase the sensitivity of those involved, first to their personhood, then to themselves as women. This new consciousness was added to the competence these women had in running their own hospitals, schools, and other institutions. When the women's movement spoke about the personhood of women, about dignity, gifts, and responsibilities, some women religious were sympathetic and often supportive. A number of nuns felt at home as participants in the movement. At the same time, they were separated from the majority of Catholic lay women. The latter had not, as a group, experienced any corresponding shift in attitudes, nor did they know much about the changes within religious life. For most lay women, the involvement of women religious in the women's movement was enigmatic and disturbing. They felt that sisters were denying their past and their life of service, that they were walking away from their religion and responsibilities.

The Opposition—A Part of the Movement

As in the past, the women's movement generated opposition from many sources. The congressional passage of the Equal Rights Amendment in 1972 served to focus much of the opposition. (See Chapter III for a more detailed look at the Equal Rights Amendment.) To many supporters of the movement, nevertheless, some of the opposition has seemed very much in step with the movement goals.

Those who claim to be participants of the women's movement know well the many contradictions and differences it harbors. Few would dispute, however, that fairly high among the movement's priorities are 1) greater opportunities for women to exercise all their gifts and talents, 2) meaningful participation of women in public life, both community life and political life, 3) public attention to issues of interest to women and 4) the development of public policy that supports women. Although organized opposition to the movement has not furthered the last mentioned goal, it has ironically done much to advance the first three. Under the aegis of organizations opposing one or another aspect of the movement, a substantial number of women have developed and exercised their many gifts. They have participated in civic and political life and they have helped draw public attention to issues of particular interest to women. Not all opposition groups encourage or even permit empowering involvement. However, to the extent that women do control the organization and do become active in the public debate, women are participating in the movement, even while opposing it.

An Agenda

The last 10 years of the women's movement has not been a period of neat, orderly growth but it has been a time of growth. A wide range of issues have mobilized women for debate and action. Older women's organizations such as the Federation of Business and Professional Women's Clubs, which asserted their separateness from the movement in the 1960s, found themselves more and more influenced by or a part of the movement in the 1970s. Professional organizations, service clubs and church women's groups have all incorporated at least a part of the movement's agenda.

What is the movement's agenda? Actually agendas would be a more accurate description, for the movement is still unorganized and those involved are sometimes working for contradictory goals. Empowerment, enabling women to take control of their own lives and to function expectively in the public arena, is one agenda item. Integration of women into public life, including public decision-making, is another. Economic equality is a third. Some women see unjust structures, particularly economic structures, as a key cause of women's oppression and want to change them. Recognition of women's gifts, talents, and needs is still another. Many women want control over their own bodies whether that control is defined as freedom from the violence of battering from spouses or of rape, pornography, freedom from the violence of battering from spouses or of rape, or freedom from unwanted pregnancies. Other women, conscious of the dichotomy between the public and private spheres and aware that humanizing values attributed to women have been confined to the private, work to move these values into the public arena in order to create a more human society. The roles of women in relationships such as marriage and family and in the work place are a concern to many women. Others focus on the principle of hierarchy and struggle to end it.

The ratification of the Equal Rights Amendmennt, to be discussed in Chapter III, is the top priority of so many groups that it can safely be listed as the leading item of the women's agenda. Unlike any other issue before the women's movement, ratification of the ERA has the support of all those who identify with the movement. Pregnancy-related issues, especially the right to abortion, might seem at a quick glance the next item on the agenda. However, a more careful look indicates that economic concerns probably rank second in priority. The specific issues range from enforcement of anti-discrimination legislation, access to jobs, and tax reforms to fairer distribution of the economic assets of a dead marriage and social security for homemakers. Equal pay for equal work and more recently equal pay for work of equal value are familiar themes to feminists. The attention of these issues reflect both the real needs of women and the value of economics in our society. Increasing numbers of women are concerned about income, taxes, credit, insurance, and so forth, becaues these issues determine their well-being and that of their families. In addition women are recognizing that their inability to influence public life is linked to their lack of money.

Much of the work of achieving economic equality for women takes place in legislatures, the courts, or within firms and organizations. These efforts usually receive little public attention. Collective action by women's groups have resulted in "Displaced Homemakers" bills that attempt to deal with the problems of older women who must become self-supporting. Women's Equity Action League and NOW Legal Defense and Education Fund have been involved in court actions that have led to improved economic situations for women. CLUW, the Coalition of Labor Union Women, is a nationwide organization of women trade unionists with goals of promoting women and women's concerns within labor unions and the spread of unionization among unorganized women workers. Women's networks, a more recent development, provides managerial women with necessary information and support structures.

Contrary to common perception, and the wishes of some activists, women who are part of the women's movement do not hold a unified view on the issue of abortion, although the issue itself is an important item on the movement's agenda. There are women, a minority to be sure, who oppose abortion under any conditions and make their views known. There are also women who talk of abortion almost as if it were a good. These women, too, represent a minority. Between these two extremes are women, who oppose abortion but are unwilling to support laws opposing it for many reasons and women who believe that at times abortion may be the lesser evil among the choices facing women. Because the abortion debate has become so polarized and bitter, and because the supports and services needed by many women are not available, many of these women who recognize abortion as an evil find themselves taking a pro-choice stance with respect to abortion laws.

The acrimonious and deep polarization over abortion, for which pro's and anti's alike are responsible, have created an almost impossible situation. Those who wish to take a qualified or nuanced position find themselves under attack from both extremes, but especially from the pro-life forces. Those who wish to raise new questions or to ask old questions from the perspectives of new insights from biology, psychology, or the social sciences, find little response. Many women, who believe that to be a part of the women's movement means an unquestioning acceptance of the right to abortion, step back from the movement despite their support of the many other issues the movement struggles with.

A wide sweep of other issues are also on the movement's agenda. Interest in ending sexist language grows out of an understanding of how words shape and limit our concepts. Studies of the differing values held by women and men reflect a concern that the values that women have traditionally nurtured not be lost but rather strengthened and embraced by all as women expand their societal roles. Child care, health, finding ways to live new roles and attitudes within family structures, exploring the links between women in developing nations and those in the US, probing history so that we might know more about women's roles and contributions: these are just some of the interests of groups that are a part of the women's movement.

Who's Who

Classifying the women and organizations that make up the women's movement makes clear how complex the movement really is. No single scheme is adequate. To focus only on the groups that are an identified part of the movement misrepresents some of the critical issues at stake. Furthermore, with few exceptions, the organizations include in their membership women who share a common concern but differ widely in their level of involvement and style of approach. Finally, style is as important as substance in distinguishing women's groups: whether a group decides to achieve its goal by education or by direct political action is often as significant as the goal itself.

With these factors in mind, I have chosen a set of categories that focus on the vision of family and society that women hold rather than specific issues before the movement. However, groups and organizations will be linked to each category. The three approaches are tradition, equality, and new society.

Tradition

The women classified as traditional and the organizations that speak in their name would, in many instances, deny being a part of the women's movement. Nevertheless, I have included them in this survey because the values they advocate are vital to our society and the world at large and need to be taken into account as the women's movement develops. In addition, the public activities of some women in the group make them very much a part of the women's movement. Phyllis Schlafly, for example, is as much known for her stand on women's issues as Betty Friedan.

Phyllis Schlafly is an interesting contradiction. She advocates traditional roles for women while her own life is that of a liberated woman complete with an accommodating husband and household and office help. She is an author, lawyer, and political activist, as well as wife and mother. Mrs. Schlafly is one model of a self-directed women, a model, that, unfortunately, she urges other women to ignore.

Traditionally-oriented women place a high value on family, community, and religion. They see the society around them changing, too often for the worse. They are, quite rightly, concerned, even fearful, of the changes. The Supreme Court decision on abortion epitomizes all that they fear. These women, however, usually do not see the connections between the changes they dislike on the one hand, and the process of industrialization, and the other structural changes on the other hand. For example, many attribute the growing number of problems facing families to the fact that women are joining the work force. Correct in seeking a link between the two, traditional women fail to recognize that women are in the work force because the economic environment requires them to be there. Other factors contribute to women's decision to be in the work force but economics is most often the determining one. Insisting that women remain full-time home-makers will not improve family life in most instances and will further harm many families by increasing the economic pressures they face. Limiting women's roles to that of homemakers also ignores women's long and proud history as producers, as well as the many gifts women are endowed with.

Our changing economic and social environment calls for new ways of living family life including more sharing of child care and household tasks and new family supports. In claiming that we must return to past practices traditional women make it more difficult to build the new forms of family and community life we need to safeguard humanizing values.

Their concerns for traditional values and practices, and their failures to see the links between changing socio-economic structures and individual issues are important reasons why traditionally-oriented women are opposed to the women's movement. These same factors also make these women very vulnerable to manipulation by people or groups favoring anti-people economic and political policies. Extreme right-wing groups have used the issues before the women's movement, such as abortion and concern about the effect of the Equal Rights Amendment, to build a political movement. For example, Phyllis Schlafly, chairperson of STOP E.R.A. and a member of the American Conservative Union, claims the ERA will strengthen the legal base supporting abortion. Knowledgeable people, such as lawyers, congresspersons, and others who have studied the amendment, have insisted that the ERA will have no effect on laws relating to abortion. Claiming that the ERA will deprive home-makers of rights as well as further the abortion cause, Mrs. Schlafly has drawn many women to STOP E.R.A. and The Eagle Forum, a membership organization she heads. In addressing the audience, Mrs. Schlafly has not only condemned the ERA and abortion, she has denounced SALT II, severely criticized efforts to improve U.S.-Soviet relations, and advocated high defense spending regardless of need or social cost.

The abortion issue lends itself to manipulation in other ways. Anti-abortion groups, using as their sole criteria a politician's stand on that one pro-life issue, have supported candidates that are anti-life, when other pro-life, pro-people issues are considered. In 1978, for example, Rep. Hyde of Illinois, author of the Hyde Amendment denying federal funding of abortions, also voted to reduce food stamps. A year earlier, in September 1977, Sen. Jesse Helms, another staunch abortion foe, was one of 11 senators voting against a bill prohibiting employers from denying pregnant women disability insurance benefits. Both these measures, and others like them, are designed to help people live. The pregnancy bill, in fact, was a direct attack on abortion since some women chose to have abortions because they could not afford the costs, including loss of all income, associated with pregnancy.

European and recent Latin American experiences amply demonstrate just how vulnerable to manipulation many traditionally-oriented women are. In Chile and Brazil, for example, the needs of the family served as a rallying call for mobilizing women to support right-wing political forces. These groups spoke of family concerns as if they were isolated from other societal problems. Upon coming to power through military coups these same rightist groups adopt policies that seriously hurt most families in their countries—policies that promote unemployment, decreased food production (by favoring agriculture for export) and separation of families (by moving living areas far from work places). To a small number of wealthier families, it seems as if family life is strengthened—their standard of living is no longer challenged. For most people, however, family life is being destroyed—and those who protest are imprisoned.

The vulnerability of traditionally-oriented women to right-wing manipulation must not, however, be used to deny these women an important voice in the women's movement. The values they champion, concern for family and children, respect for life, an appreciation of community, of decency, and of service are values that enrich and humanize life. Somehow, if it is to grow, the women's movement must find ways to nourish these values while creating a society that treats women justly. To achieve this goal, traditionally-oriented women must come to see their concerns within the context of a changing society and the women's movement must acknowledge the importance of values it has tended to ignore.

Equality

The mainstream of the current phase of the women's movement accepts the basic economic and political tenets of U.S. society and seeks primarily to be included equally in that society. The organizations and the courses of action they have adopted are directly in line with the dominant political ideology of 20th-Century United States—liberalism. Traditionally, liberalism has tackled problems facing our society by 1) identifying and isolating the problem not only from other issues but also from its historical and societal context, 2) setting a goal or goals that will indicate that the problem has been solved; often these goals do not take into account the social environment in which they are to be achieved and 3) developing the tactics and strategies that will achieve the objectives set. Because of this style, liberalism, in its problem-solving, tends to fragment society—setting one or another group over against the whole.

The women's movement is the true daughter of the liberal perspective. The discriminatory treatment of women has been clearly identified as the problem. The goal of the movement is to provide for equal treatment of women in every aspect of societal life. Legal, legislative, and educational strategies have been adopted. However, this mainstream of the women's movement, like more traditional groups, has failed to link many of the movement's separate goals with the structures that shape our society.

It is only recently, that some movement advocates have come to recognize the profound systemic changes that will take place if women do achieve equality. For example, the relationships between family and community will shift once again. In pre-industrial times, family ties, geography and shared needs linked family and community tightly. The whole family contributed to building community. In industrial societies both family and community have suffered, especially community. Responsibility for what community life exists has fallen to women who, because they are home, seem to have some time for building relationships. With women in the work force, we are going to have to develop new mechanisms for fostering community, mechanisms that involve men as well as women. Otherwise, community life will further disintegrate.

The failure of the women's movement to see itself in a systematic context, especially during its formation, has created some serious problems for the movement. Many movement activists minimized the value of homemaking, while struggling to affirm women and open new opportunities for them, especially in the public arena. They also tended to display a great deal of impatience with women who chose traditional roles, in effect, setting women against women. As a consequence, many homemakers were alienated from the movement. As it matured, however, and more women joined, the movement recognized the narrow, even contradictory position it was taking if while advocating choice for women it discredited homemaking. Some feminists, in addition, pointed out the many benefits homemakers brought to our society. Though not unanimous, a substantial shift to supporting homemakers has taken place. It has not, however, received the media attention that the previous negative attitude received.

The shift in the movement's response to homemaking is one indication of the makeup of mainstream organizations. NOW, Women's Equity Action League, Women's Political Caucus, and similar organizations embrace a wide national constituency. That constituency includes women holding traditional views about the roles of women, yet concerned about the discrimination against women, some who want to see the society completely changed by the efforts of women, as well as those who want to see full equality for women within the existing system. As these organizations strive to meet the needs of their constituencies, they find themselves pressed to understand the relationships among issues. This has been especially true for NOW. In recent years, the organization's leadership and a significant portion of its membership have studied problems and advocated policies that have linked issues. Whether or not it can continue to do this and maintain its size as the nation as a whole moves to a more conservative position because of slowed economic growth is a question only the future can answer.

One further comment needs to be made about the makeup of

mainstream groups of this phase of the women's movement. Not all women's organizations see themselves as women's rights, or women's movement groups. The YMCA, the Girl Scouts, church-related groups and many other organizations have a history and interests that extend beyond what is ordinarily thought of as the women's movement. However, to the extent that these groups do advocate women's rights, most would belong to this substantial grouping of liberally-oriented women's groups.

Style has been as important a question to the women's movement as substance. Where does one put one's energy; lobbying in Congress or the state legislature, seeking court action to redress wrongs, or meeting the needs of one or another group of women directly? NOW engages in all these activities. Others focus on one or another cluster of needs and develop an approach that seems appropriate.

Style has also been a cause of criticism for the movement. Often this criticism reflects the "can't win" situation that women themselves are in. Women have found that if they do not speak up they do not achieve the goals that are important to them. If they do speak up they are labeled aggressive, overbearing, angry. If women's meetings are run in a non-hierarchical way, they are criticized for being unorganized. If they are run in a more conventional manner, they are criticized for being just like men's meetings, or undemocratic, or contentious and fragmented. There is little space for trying out new styles—for it seems as if we as a nation want certain levels of efficiency and perfection but are unwilling to give people and processes the time to develop.

The question of style becomes important when trying to classify groups. Is a group radical/far out/ahead of its time because it explores and fosters ideas that are not commonly considered in the society—new forms of relationships between men and women, new ideas about the ownership of property? Or is the group radical because in addition to lobbying for change, participating in many community activities and sponsoring activities and women's centers that meet the specific needs of women, it uses rallies, marches, and public demonstrations to publicize its stand?

For most of us, especially those who grew up before the 1960s, marches, public rallies and demonstrations are disturbing, suspect forms of behavior. It had been a long while since the U.S. had seen any similar activities—the 1930s probably. We have forgotten that throughout history, public demonstrations have been a part of politics. Ordinary people have turned to the streets to protest when the normal political channels no longer work. Sometimes the protest has been under the guise of a religious procession—the response to Pope John Paul II in Poland is a good example. Sometimes it's been a riot carrying with it the seeds for further anger and bitterness. Usually, however, people have chosen non-violent marches and rallies to mobilize support and call attention to the need for change.

It's easy to label public demonstrations radical. Many have. This label, however, is not very useful since the ideas and policies a group supports are as important as the tactics it adopts. Labeling a group on the basis of tactics alone is a way to avoid responding to their ideas. And too often this has been the way a government or powerful group in society has quickly covered over a real and serious injustice.

Amost all the women's groups that are large enough to hold public demonstrations fall into the mainstream of U. S. societal thought. NOW, the Coalition of Labor Union Women, Women's Equity Action League, religious groups, National Women's Political Caucus, and many other groups are willing to join in some marches and rallies. Yet, in terms of the ideas and policies they advocate, these groups are not radical. They ask only that U.S. women be included equally in U.S. society.

Promoters of a New Society

From the beginning there have been persons and groups within the women's movement who have advanced bits and pieces of a new vision of society. Some have sought new ways of structuring public institutions and businesses. More have explored new forms of relationships within marriage, and family patterns that respect the gifts and abilities of each spouse, forms that encourage individual growth. These new family patterns, for example, have varied from real efforts to share household and child-care responsibilities to efforts at community living. A few women have argued that marriage is no longer a viable institution and should be done away with. (This extreme position is refuted by all those who live the benefits of a good and happy marriage. However, this and similar arguments cannot be dismissed precipitously for they pinpoint some of the places of pressure and pain that afflict marriages today. In a sense, even the most negative idea could contribute to strengthening the institution of marriage.)

A second contribution to the new vision comes out of the efforts to probe feminine attitudes, experiences, and history, and to discover and understand feminine styles of behavior, values, and philosophies. The insight gained from this aspect of the women's movement could have a very humanizing effect on all relationships, and on the way we organize public life. Those who are seeking to know more about the feminine are finding traditions and attitudes that support cooperation, participation and empowerment, as opposed to competition and unrelated individualism. They fear that former values will be lost as women struggle to become equal in our society. The challenge they face, the one they present to all of us, is how to preserve the positive humanizing values they have identified while at the same time affirming the variety of experiences, gifts and needs of individual women—all within the context of significant societal change.

Part of the answer lies in the study and proposals of the women and men who are looking more closely at the structures that shape our society. These people have shown that the process of industrialization as it has taken place in the West has eroded the traditional roles and responsibilities of women. They have also pointed out that increased automation and the global movement of capital and industry, that is leading to unemployment and inflation, are putting great pressures on moderate and low-income families and individuals. These pressures, which include fragmentation and alienation within the society and family and new questions about education methods and goals as well as worry about money, will not be reduced easily.

The women who share the analysis are advocating both short-range and long-term responses. In the short-range they seek greater opportunities for women, especially in the work force. They are urging women to organize at the work place and in the neighborhood to obtain better services—day care, health, education. For the long run they are stressing the need for women and men to analyze what is happening to them and their society, to participate in institutions with an aim of making them more responsive to people's needs, and where necessary and possible, to form alternative institutions. The advocates of this position set the women's movement within a global perspective, and attempt to identify the links between global and national events and happenings at the local level.

As in other approaches to the women's movement, the promoters of a new society draw their inspiration from a variety of sources. Some, acting on the belief that women and men are equal to each other, seek to build a new society through the cooperation of men and women. Others, agreeing with the need for cooperation, find the elements of their vision in socialism, that is a political and economic system that advocates democracy not only on political issues but on economic issues as well.

The groups that are trying to promote a new vision for the society include small church-related groups such as the Women, Work and the Economy Project of Theology in the Americans. (Theology in the Americas is an ecumenical project, drawing its inspiration from the liberation school of theology. The project facilitates small groups in their effort to analyze their situation and reflect upon this analysis in the light of scripture.) Groups at universities and in some women's centers have also contributed to the new vision. The development of a socialist perspective is on the agenda of groups of socialist feminists who are often members of national socialist organizations, such as the Democratic Socialist Organizing Committee, a socialist group within the Democratic party, and the New America Movement, a socialist outgrowth of the student movements of the 1960s. All of these groups though small are often linked by an informal network that promotes the sharing of concerns and ideas.

These groups join in marches, rallies and public demonstrations, but most devote their primary efforts to a combination of self-education, community education, and service. The writings of women promoters of a new vision place new ideas and insights before the women's movement and the community at large.

As mentioned above, one of the problems with classifying the organiziations that make up the women's movement is that the members of any organization represent a spectrum of views. Many women who strive to promote a new vision for our society are members of mainstream organizations and at times they do influence these organizations. The reverse is also true. Women seeking only equality become members of an organization seeking a new vision, often because the group is the only one available or because it is particularly effective in achieving a specific goal.

The Future

What will happen to this second phase of the women's movement? Will it unite to pass the ERA and then die? Will it be defeated in its efforts and disappear? Will it be a significant factor in building a more human and just society?

The agenda of the women's movement is broad and touches issues important to women and to society as a whole. It is unlikely that its future will be limited to the ERA or that it will go away. However, the role the movement will play in the shaping of our society is an open question. If the movement can combine the insights and understandings it has gained about women, their experiences and their gifts with the values that have traditionally been the concern of women in a way that responds to the pressures generated by new societal structures, it will be a significant factor in shaping our future. The task is big. It means that women will have to study carefully the past to separate the value—whether it be a strong family life or volunteering to serve the community—from the way that value was practiced in a particular time and place. They will have to join with men to make that value viable in a society which not only experiences changes and conflict, but also seeks justice. Building that just society requires the effort of the whole human community.

Suggested Readings

Maren Lockwood Carden, *The New Feminist Movement* (Russell Sage Foundation, New York, 1974).
Feminism in the Mid-1970s (Ford Foundation, New York, 1977).
Studies in the history and structure of the organizations that make up the U.S. Women's Movement.

William Chafe, *Women and Equality: Changing Patterns in American Culture* (Oxford University Press, New York, 1977).
A history of women's struggle for equality in the United States which includes a critical comparison of women's efforts with black peoples' struggle for justice.

Eleanor Flexner, *Century of Struggle* (Harvard University Press, Cambridge, Massachusetts, 1959).
A highly respected history of the early phase of the U.S. Women's Movement which gained for women the right to vote.

Jo Freeman, *The Politics of Women's Liberation* (David McKay Company Inc., New York, 1975).
An examination of the U.S. Women's Movement as a social movement with political ramifications.

3.
THE ERA: POTENTIAL FOR WHAT?

The Equal Rights Amendment to the U.S. Constitution

Section 1.
Equality of rights under the law shall not be denied or abridged by the United States or by any state on account of sex.

Section 2.
The Congress shall have the power to enforce, by appropriate legislation, the provisions of this article.

Section 3.
This amendment shall take effect two years after the date of ratification.

Proponents claim that the ERA will open up the world to women; opponents claim it will remove all the protections women have and destroy marriage. The evidence, however, indicates that the ERA will not open up the world but it will structure it so that women can open it up for themselves. It will not remove all women's protections and destroy marriage; rather it will provide some new protections and promote a new mutuality in marriage.

It Will and It Won't: A Story

Anna Plank,* an almost 40-year-old mother of three, was having late morning coffee with her visiting aunt and mother. The two older women, sisters, looked alike but were as different as the bananas

---

*This dialogue and the stories of women throughout the text are fictionalized accounts of actual happenings.

and apples in the center of the table. Joan Costa, the younger by 10 years, was outgoing, even argumentative, and usually willing to try something different. After college, she had married an easy-going engineer who died 20 years later leaving her with happy memories, four children, and not enough money. Now, after 15 years the children have children of their own and Joan had a demanding and adequately paying job in a greenhouse-nursery. She seemed pleased with herself and her not always easy life. Alice Brent's life had been more orderly, predictable. She was a quiet, capable, and usually confident woman who, she would admit, had some definite opinions that she made known to family and close friends. She had married at 20 a man who just this year retired as a successful sales manager. Money had been no concern to Alice as she raised her three children: Anna was her oldest. When the children were on their own, she became a volunteer at the local hospital but had recently stopped. It didn't bring the satisfaction it once did.

The morning mail had started the argument. A brightly colored newsletter from the South Shore Women's Center sat on the top of the pile. Its lead article reported on the status of the ERA. Alice Brent's acid comment that she hoped Anna did not belong to any group supporting that amendment brought a quick challenging rejoinder from her sister. Joan Costa insisted that the ERA was the best thing that could ever happen to women.

At first Anna felt the usual strain between not wanting another fruitless argument with her mother and not wanting to be less than truthful. But as she listened to the two women, who seemed to forget she was there, she found herself more and more disturbed by their claims and counterclaims. Her aunt seemed to believe that once the ERA was passed all women's problems would automatically end. Her mother repeated every objection to the ERA that Anna had ever heard and some new ones.

The two women paused, Anna filled the coffee cups, took a long sip from her own and decided to forget she was daughter and niece and spell out a more realistic picture of the Equal Rights Amendment.

Telling her aunt her turn was coming, she reminded her mother that she had always insisted that her children get the facts straight. Now, Anna announced, was getting-facts-straight time. Twice her mother had talked about the homosexual marriages in Colorado, but admitted under Anna's questioning that she didn't think anyone claimed it was legal. Anna, as her aunt's face recorded uneasiness with this approach, filled in some facts for her mother. In the early 1970s a local marriage bureau clerk issued licenses to men after consulting with a local district attorney. The State Attorney General held the licenses were invalid when he learned they had been issued. In 1972 Colorado had a state ERA and it has been assumed that the clerk issued the licenses because of that law. In fact, the clerk believed the long-existing state marriage law authorized him to do so. However, ERA opponents, who know better, keep repeating the story and its false assumptions. States define marriage as occurring between a man and a woman, Anna reminded her mother. Since both men and women are treated equally, the ERA cannot be used as a basis for giving legal sanctions to a relationship between homosexuals.

Mrs. Brent just glared at her daughter—then noticed the tease in her voice as Anna asked her when she'd last used a unisex toilet. "Stop teasing," Joan Costa blurted, "you know very well privacy laws don't allow them and anyway there isn't any conflict between the ERA and privacy."

Anna suppressed a laugh as she began quoting the two women's review of their trip the night they arrived. "Airplanes—I don't mind the narrow aisles but those seats,"—"I felt like I was sitting in a child's chair." "And the bathroom—why if I weighed 10 pounds more I'd be in real trouble." "I felt real sorry for the man waiting behind me—he had two small boys." All three women began laughing. Maryland with it's state ERA had a number of questions about unisex bathrooms, Anna mentioned. There'd been a report of some in schools, denied by an angry school official. The Golden Seal Builders Inc. thought they could save themselves some money by citing the ERA when they submitted building plans for a shopping mall with only one restroom per store. They couldn't, and they redrew their plans before they received their building permit.

Mrs. Brent was a little surprised at her daughter; Anna had never talked back, no, up, to her before. But the ERA will force homemakers to go to work she insisted—"Just wait, when that law is passed you'll have to go to work." "That is hogwash," said Anna in a tone of aggravated exasperation. The ERA affects only laws, it does not regulate the private relationships between people, she reminded both women. Both parents have always supported children, she added, usually the father with his earnings, the mother with care and other non-monetary supports. In all the talk about the ERA, not many people have noticed that it has been the women's movement that has kept stressing the non-monetary contributions of women to family life. STOP E.R.A. and similar groups keep talking about support as if it were money only. Where there are state equal rights amendments, the courts have adopted the women's movement perspective in dealing with divorce settlements—women's non-monetary contributions to marriage and family life are being recognized. Divorce settlements in Pennsylvania and Texas, for example, have specifically cited these non-monetary necessities.

Anna slowly began telling the two other women of a couple of neighborhood divorces. Both marriages seemed successful and stable so the divorces themselves had shaken Anna and some of her friends. Their dismay was compounded when they learned of the settlements. Because their state had no equal rights amendment, the courts relied on traditional concepts in dividing up the property. Both women received the house but not enough money to insure they would be able to keep it. The younger woman received an alimony award for three years—long enough to establish herself, the judge had observed. No attention was given to the problems she would face as a 40-year-old woman with little work experience and two teenagers to care for. The other woman, Mrs. Collins, was in her late 50s. The alimony she was receiving was barely sufficient to cover mortgage payments. This woman's situation was particularly painful, for she had been married 35 years, and never worked outside the home. She had expected that her husband's pension would provide for her. Now she would receive some coverage under Social Security, new regulations provided that, but she would not receive a share of the more substantial private pension. Anna and her neighbors shared the woman's feelings that her willingness and ability to manage on a reduced income had made that pension possible. But that didn't matter; Mrs. Collins now alone, has had to start building her future.

Anna looked at the clock, decided it was well worth postponing the laundry to continue this talk and warmed up the coffee. The experience of her divorced neighbors had been an education to Anna in many ways. Not only had it made her acutely conscious of how vulnerable women were, but it had also made her aware of the potential and limits of the ERA. Far from being a federal grab for power, Anna feared it would not provide enough protection. Her aunt demanded to know what she meant.

Anna asked her aunt what would happen if, after the amendment were ratified, people just sat back and expected it to be effective, if people ceased being sensitive to sexism because of a law saying it was unconstitutional. Mrs. Costa commented that that was silly, that it wouldn't happen that way. Anna hoped she was right. However, federal courts decide which cases they would hear and not hear. Crowded calendars, lack of money to properly prepare cases, and an absence of interested lawyers were still barriers to be overcome. Courts often reflected local attitudes and practices; how would the courts in those states where the ERA had not been ratified respond? As for her own state, Anna was now convinced of the need for a state ERA. The federal amendment was vital, but without a state amendment women would possibly still find themselves unfairly treated in divorce proceedings and similar situations for a long time to come. Both older women were surprised; her aunt seemed deflated. Anna's response was a quick assurance that ratification of the ERA would make a difference. If men and women were treated equally by laws, women's situations in education, health care, employment, and so many other areas including criminal justice and welfare would improve. The changes in practice, to match the laws, however, would not always be automatic or peaceful, especially in the area of family law. It would take time and testing to find ways of combining equality and other values.

Suddenly Mrs. Brent shifted in her chair. "The ERA," she inserted, "will further increase the number of abortions." Anna shook her head slowly. "They are two separate and distinct issues related only because women are involved." "Since men can't have babies women will want to be treated equally and not have babies," was her mother's response. "Since men don't bear children and women do, applying the Equal Rights Amendment to child-bearing is silly and illogical," answered Anna. "The Equal Rights Amendment deals with equal treatment of men and women by laws. Laws do not decree that women have chidlren and men not; human anatomy does. Laws can't change that. What's more," noted Anna, "confusing the issue has only made dealing with both issues more difficult."

"The whole range of pregnancy and abortion issues needs thoughtful, sympathetic attention. How are we going to deal with pregnant teenagers, just to start? Mixing the ERA and abortion has not ended abortion and seems to be a self-defeating tactic."

"What about the draft?" snapped Mrs. Brent. "What about it?" answered Anna. "With or without the ERA, women will probably be drafted in the near future; there just isn't going to be that big pool of young men from which to draw." Anna admitted that the idea of women in combat wasn't something she liked either, although she confessed, in terms of personality, it looked like her daughter would cope better with military life than her older son. Anna brought up another point. "New styles of warfare were wiping out many of the distinctions between soldiers and civilians. In fact, civilians seem more vulnerable than soldiers. They lacked the training and the means for defending themselves, they suffered the shortages, their homes were destroyed in bombings. Women and children, especially, were more and more the casualties of war. This has been the experience of most recent wars. Maybe girls would be safer in the military than at home." Anna grinned, "And remember," she said, "I'm opposed to the draft, period—and I believe our military budget is too large. But that's another argument. I'm afraid with or without the ERA women will be involved in combat if there is a future war."

It was quiet, then Mrs. Brent commented, "You sound so logical and so sure of yourself, but I still can't approve of the ERA. It's just one more thing that's changing our society, making trouble for families," Anna nodded. "You've put your finger on something," she said. "Our society is changing. Things are more hectic. People are more separated, more puzzled, less confident and hopeful. But the ERA isn't a cuase of all that. It's a response—one that will at least give women the opportunity to catch up. So blaming it for the changes won't stop them. That will only keep us from finding and dealing wisely with the real cause of change. And that hurts all of us." She paused, then added, "You think about it, I've got to get the laundry started—and it's just about time for lunch."

The ERA: What It Is and Why It is Important

A Legal Statement

The Equal Rights Amendment is a law about other laws. If ratified it will make unconstitutional those laws that discriminate against persons based on sex. The ERA will insure that the rest of the constitution applies equally to women and men. The ERA will mean—to use the legal term—that sex will be a suspect category, that any legal discrimination will require "strict scrutiny" by the courts before being upheld.

The history of court rulings to date clearly shows that the court cannot make up its mind about the legal equality of men and women. Until 1971, moreover, the Supreme Court never viewed discrimination against women as a violation of the equal protection clause of the 14th Amendment, the clause so often cited by those who claim we don't need an ERA. Since 1971 the record has been inconsistent.

Sharron A. Frontiero, an Air Force lieutenant, listed her husband as a dependent in order to claim the many benefits the military provides servicemen's wives. The Air Force said she could not do this. In 1973 the Supreme Court ruled (*Frontiero vs. Richardson*) that the then current military practice of denying benefits to servicewomen's husbands was unconstitutional. However, the Court disagreed on why it was unconstitutional, so the ruling left many questions. Four years later the same court ruled that the law prohibiting Susan Vorskheimer from attending a one-of-a-kind, elite public technical high school in Philadelphia solely because she was a girl was allowable. The Equal Rights Amendment will end the confusion and wavering by stating clearly that women and men are equal before the law.

The Amendment will serve as a backup to insure that recently enacted laws calling for equal treatment of men and women under a variety of specific circumstances will not be changed in the future to favor persons of one sex over those of another. Although it may now seem unlikely that Congress or state legislatures would reverse laws providing for women's access to credit, equal pay for equal work, or the many other laws insuring women's equal protection by the law, reversal is possible. Where equality is economically costly there will be pressures for change or exemptions, especially during those times when there is little economic growth.

Ratification of the ERA will provide the opportunity and the necessity for states to review all their laws from the perspective of sexism. Without an ERA existing laws that discriminate against women will be examined one by one as they are challenged in the courts. Not only is this a time-consuming process, but it is costly. Furthermore, it often denies justice to the poorer women in our society who lack the resources in money, access to legal help, and time to pursue a case through courts. Public legal services organizations like the Women's Equity Action League or the National Association for the Advancement of Colored People, have limited resources and so must set priorities about the cases they accept.

When the ERA is finally ratified, there will be a two-year period before it becomes effective. That time was provided in order to allow the states the time needed to review and rewrite laws. Many laws can easily be changed. Some, lawmakers will discover, are obsolete and need to be repealed. Some laws will be difficult to rewrite and will need attention from both lawyers and the community. Other laws will shift the focus to the function or event rather than the sex of the person involved. For example, in those states where rape laws are written in such a way as to focus on women, the victims, the laws will be rewritten to focus on assault, the crime involved. This action alone will probably help reduce rape, for it confronts the blame-the-victim approach now common in dealing with rape. Family law and work protection laws will also need careful attention. What does the community want the laws to do? Are they now needed? Should employment-related protection laws be extended to cover both women and men? Some laws will involve changes in costs. How will the community respond? Some of the changes will, quite rightly, generate a lot of attention and discussion.

The ERA will also provide some measure of evenness in the treatment of women throughout the nation. Job opportunities, employment itself, health concerns, retirement, even dreams, all encourage individuals, couples, and families to move about the country. Women find that the rights they have vary markedly from state to state. In some states local laws back federal employment laws. In other states, local laws discriminate against women, and the agencies designed to enforce federal laws are reluctant to act. This unevenness places added burdens on women who must move.

Finally, the ERA will put some force behind the myriad of regulations, city, state and federal, designed to bring about legal equal treatment of women. At present there are laws and regulations inadequately enforced because they are a low priority for those who are supposed to implement them. As long as the nation only debates about the equality of men and women, many administrators, inspectors, and so forth, whose responsibility it is to monitor and enforce these rules, will feel that the nation is not serious in its attack on sexism. They will direct their limited resources to areas of demonstrated public concern.

Who Will Be Affected?

Because there is an interplay between law and society, the ERA will, over time, have social effects on us as persons and as a community. The equality of women under the law will sanction the equal treatment of women and men in other situations. Proponents have had to agree, reluctantly, with opponents that they don't know exactly what this will mean. However, there are some guides. The civil rights legislation, for example, has eased social relationships between the black and white communities yet it has not led to the integrated society that some had hoped for and others feared. There are places where people are making a conscious effort to reduce racial barriers while still respecting and nurturing cultural differences. However, some people, black and white, find the civil rights acts touch only a part of their lives. And probably for the majority of white families the acts have had no effect on either their economic or social situation.

It is safe to say that the Equal Rights Amendment will affect different groups of people in very dissimilar ways. For many, it won't make much noticeable difference. This is especially true for older women and men whose lives are stable and who have some economic security. The improved Social Security benefits women will eventually receive will enrich their lives more, but won't make a significant difference. Poorer older women, however, will notice the impact of fairer Social Security regulations.

Married, middle-aged women who are not a part of the work force won't find their lives changed too much either—unless they are divorced or widowed. Then, they will find themselves in a stronger economic position than they would be without an ERA. If the Social Security system is modified to take into account the economic value of homemakers' work, a goal of the women's movement, these women will be assured of greater financial security as they grow older. They will benefit as well from the general improvement in the status of women.

The ERA will, over time, make important differences to younger people and women in the work force. The latter will have to speak up and claim their equality. However, the existence of an ERA will give social as well as legal supports to claims for equal opportunities. It will ease the process of restructuring work to accommodate women, and in the process make work more responsive to people's lives rather than, as is the present case, force people to accommodate work.

Young people, already struggling with the issues of sexual equality, both on the job and in their private lives, will continue to contend with the tensions that are a part of balancing equality with family and community needs. The ratification of the ERA will intensify the tensions while providing support for people's efforts for fairer treatment of women.

Probably not our children but maybe our grandchildren will reap the full benefits of an Equal Rights Amendment. Both girls and boys will have the opportunity to develop their full potential. Neither will be hobbled by sex-based stereotypes. This does not deny that there are differences between male and female but rather acknowledges that men and women, girls and boys are much more alike than they are different.

Many people actively committed to equality between men and women and the Equal Rights Amendment are already exploring ways of fitting together equality and our essential institutions. How does a couple who see themselves as equal share home chores and child care? If more women are in the work force what will happen to children—what kinds of day care do we need? And what of extended-family relationships? Many pressures—jobs, distances, new forms of entertainment, small spaces—mitigate against strong extended families. Yet, more and more couples are making some hard decisions in favor of building roots and staying close to relatives. Men and women are foregoing promotions, taking less exciting jobs, even lesser-paying jobs because to do otherwise would further fragment their family. The fear that equality will destroy our humanness does not seem justified. We will have to work for our institutions and values; we will have to find new ways of living them out, but with or without an ERA we will have to do that.

Global Impact

The international impact of a United States Equal Rights Amendment is rarely considered in debates over the amendment. Nevertheless, the United States serves as a leader and model in the global community. This is especially true from the perspective of the women's movement. The fact that U.S. women live in a materially better situation than women in many other parts of the world is recognized universally. The ability of U.S. women to organize and articulate their demands makes the American women's movement, with all its virtues and faults, highly visible.

The United States is one of a few nations that does not secure the legal equality of men and women in its basic law. This fact has not gone unnoticed. Often the struggle for justice by women in other parts of the world is dismissed by local policymakers through invidious comparisons with the situation of U.S. women. The presence of an article of equality in the national law, even if unenforced, is cited along with characteristics of the U.S. movement that are alien to local culture. For these policy makers the absence of an equal rights statement in the U.S. constitution confirms their belief that U.S. men, the powerbrokers, believe women to be unimportant, inferior beings who can safely be ignored. The ratification of the Equal Rights Amendment would be a significant statement that the United States does in fact take women and their struggle for complete personhood seriously.

The History of the ERA

Beginnings

Alice Paul, one of the women who organized the suffrage marches in Washington, wrote the first Equal Rights Amendment shortly after women won the right to vote. The amendment was introduced in Congress in 1923 by the National Women's Party. It immediately became the focus of strong opposition. To most Americans of the 1920s the idea that men and women are equal, was a non-issue. Some people agreed in theory that women and men are equal, but not many felt any need to put theory into practice. Most people thought of women and men in terms of roles and most believed those roles to be very different. Among the many objections raised, two seem to have stood out: the ERA would overturn the painfully won protective legislation designed to safeguard women in the workplace and to promote the health and well-being of mothers; and the ERA would destroy marriage.

The debate over the ERA centered on the issue of protective legislation. Women who had fought for suffrage but believed in the need for protective legislation were joined by women who had fought against it. Members of the National Women's Party, which had introduced the amendment, argued that if the protections and benefits, such as restrictions on overtime, night work, or on weights an individual could lift, were needed, they were needed by men as well as women and should be extended. Otherwise, the Party claimed, such laws would only work to women's disadvantage by excluding them from significant job opportunities. Labor Department studies showed that, at least with regard to unskilled workers, the Party argument was correct; women were being denied jobs they had previously held because of one or another law. Women were forced out of the printing industry, for example, because they could not work nights, when most of the work was done.

Even so, the prevailing attitude, voiced by those who had initiated and supported the protective legislation, was that losses women sustained because of legal restrictions were more than offset by the benefits they gained. The creation of women-dominated, low-paying job areas was an unfortunate but acceptable by-product. Industry could not and would not extend the protections to men, it was argued. Women would lose all if the ERA was passed.

The arguments about the ERA's effect on protective legislation was backed by arguments about its destructive impact on marriage. Then, as now, many felt it would undermine the laws that required men to support their families. In addition, they claimed it would require women to make an equal financial contribution to the family. By taking away the protection and special rights of mothers it would also harm children.

Public support for the bill did not increase even though it was introduced in every Congress after 1923. Despite congressional hearings, it faded from public view as American women directed almost all their attention to being wives and mothers and to coping with the Depression and World War II. The late 1940s and early 1950s brought some renewed interest. In 1950 and again in 1953 the Senate passed the amendment with the "Hayden rider" attached, which provided that "the provisions of this article shall not be construed to impair any rights, benefits and exemptions now or hereafter conferred by law upon persons of the female sex." In the eyes of ERA supporters this clause effectively negated the amendment itself.

On to the Women's Agenda

The ERA came slowly and was unwelcomed on the agenda of phase two of the women's movement. As mentioned earlier NOW's support of the amendment was a key factor in the decision of some members to form a new organization, Women's Equity Action League (WEAL), in 1968. Today WEAL is one of the foremost promoters of the ERA. Although the support for the amendment did grow, some segments of the public, such as the labor unions and some church groups, did not become supporters until after it was passed by the House on a vote of 354 to 23 in October 1971, by the Senate on a vote of 84 to 8 five months later and sent on to the states for ratification.

One year after the ERA had been submitted to the states, 30 had ratified it. At that point the rate of ratification slowed, and the amendment, as of this writing, is three states short of ratification. The extension of the ratification deadline voted by Congress in 1978 means that the U.S. public has until June 30, 1982 to finish ratifying it.

Revival—Why?

A fair question to ask about the ERA might be why after almost 50 years did it become acceptable in the early 1970s. Is the women's movement responsible for its current popularity, or has something else changed?

Opponents and proponents alike may hold the women's movement responsible for the ERA; however, that is only part of the story. The changing social fabric—a high divorce rate, need for more education, inflation, longer lives, to name just a few of the recent changes—has caused many women to reach for rights they had always assumed were theirs but which they did not need previously. They assumed, for example, that husbands and inheritance laws would treat them fairly, that ability determines how far one gets on a job. Women have learned their assumptions are wrong, and they are telling others what's really happening.

Jane Schmidt of Nebraska and her new husband Bill bought a farm just before World War II. For 30 years they worked the farm together—except during World War II when Jane worked it alone. Bill died suddenly in 1968. Much to her surprise and dismay, Jane found herself responsible for inheritance taxes on the farm. In 1968 both the state and federal government disallowed her claim that her work input qualified her as a part owner. Much against her will, and contrary to the dreams she and Bill shared, Jane had to sell the farm. The hurt grew when Jane realized that if she had died, Bill would not have faced the same taxes.

Mary Russo went back to work as a laboratory technician in a metal fabricating plant because the family needed money to cover increasing school costs. She was good at her job, and felt proud when asked to train new technicians. She also felt she was capable of doing more demanding work. She began to grow angry when each of the young men she trained was promoted while she and other women were still doing the low-skilled, low-paying jobs. Her questions about the fairness of this practice resulted in a threat of being fired. The income from the job is important to her family, and jobs are scarce, so Mary Russo has said no more about a promotion.

Ann Paulson became an ERA supporter after her neighbor Ellen Chaney was killed. The Chaneys had married in their 30s and had three small children who were clearly very important to both. Joe tried a variety of ways to care for the children while he worked, all unsatisfactory. He finally decided that if he claimed survivor benefits, designed to assure children of adequate care, under Ellen's Social Security and worked part-time he would have enough money for the family and be able to care for the children as Ellen would have wanted. But, according to the Social Security regulations at the time, Joe was not eligible for benefits even though his wife had paid into Social Security for over 15 years. Anne Paulson and her neighbors talked about the unfairness of this and about their vulnerability. Anne and six of her friends became very vocal ERA supporters.

Other experiences of women in the work force also generated much support for the amendment. Women found that even though entry skills were the same, there were two tracks within many firms. One led to training, promotions and well-paying jobs—men were on that track. The other involved no training, few promotions and jobs that paid relatively little—women were on that track. Other women found that even though night shifts best fitted their family care situation and financial needs, protective legislation excluded them from the jobs. Still others found that restrictions on the jobs women could hold based upon strength differences between men and women were increasingly meaningless. New technology had replaced the need for strength. Often the jobs they were barred from were those at the beginning of a chain of better jobs that depended more on skill and know-how than brawn. In many places, retail stores, schools, bakeries, and so forth, women began to see that the customary pattern of women workers being supervised by men just didn't make sense; that women were as capable as men and deserved positions of responsibility and authority. All of these, women sought to change.

Slowly the situation of women began to improve. The Civil Rights Act of 1964 barred discrimination in employment on the basis of sex. Women, as well as blacks, began to demand that government enforce the law and to initiate law suits against employers they felt were violating the law. Affirmative action programs were a consequence of these activities. Employers, often under the directive of the Federal Government, developed a program of actions that would in theory eliminate discrimination against women in the work force.

A change of attitude on the part of the leadership of trade unions also helped improve the conditions of working women. Union women demanded support from the leadership for their issues and also questioned the decision of many unions to oppose the ERA. First at the local level, and finally at the national, the unions began to talk of women's rights and to support the ERA.

The affirmative action programs, themselves, led to significant ERA support. Women involved with the programs, either as staff or job seekers, found in many instances that the program was a sham. Not only were those in positions of authority unwilling to support the spirit of the effort, but these same people let it be known that they felt affirmative action to be a passing fad. If businesses and institutions just delayed long enough, many believed, women would go back to being housewives and secretaries. Government officials charged with supervising affirmative action programs often felt the same way. The Equal Rights Amendment, many came to see, would serve notice that the nation really was committed to equality for women.

Many women and men who did not expect their lives to be changed in any way by the amendment became supporters because they wanted their children, both daughters and sons, to have opportunities they themselves did not have because of sexism. Others, becoming conscious of the many ways both men and women are penalized because of sexism also began working for its ratification. Church-related women were a part of all of these groups. Hesitantly, then more strongly, the church organizations to which these women belonged began to support the amendment. However, not all church-related women's organizations support the ERA; Mormon women, those belonging to fundamentalist churches, and the National Council of Catholic Women, for example, firmly oppose it. Nevertheless, the backing of church-related women has been an important source of active advocacy for the amendment.

The Ratification Effort

Securing state ratification of the Equal Rights Amendment and the passage of state ERAs has been both exciting and shattering for many of the women involved. Women who ten years ago knew little about politics have become experts in legislative committees, sub-committees, seniority and the "good ole boy" network.

Facing the stalling tactic of state legislators (there are still legislatures where the ERA has not reached the floor of one or another house), women moved into electoral politics and learned an additional lesson. In Nevada, North Carolina and Florida, for example, legislators who spoke out for the ERA while running for office voted against it. Some of these "gentlemen" had accepted the support, both money and workers, of pro-ERA groups during their campaign.

The defeat of referenda for state equal rights amendments in New York and New Jersey in 1975 served as another kind of lesson to ERA proponents. Post-election analysis made clear the proponents had not paid much attention to the concerns of middle- and working-class homemakers, especially their concerns about the fragmentation of the family and the erosion of family support. Opponents of the amendment had built a well-organized and funded campaign on the fears of these women and soundly defeated the amendment.

After watching their electoral work come to nothing because the ERA never reached the floor for a vote of the full legislature, women in Northern Virginia decided that a change in leadership was necessary. In 1977 VERA-PAC, a pro-ERA coalition, targeted House Majority Leader James M. Thomson for replacement by candidate Gary R. Myers, who, in addition to supporting public transportation, a major issue in the area, favored the ERA. The women won. Thomson lost in an election that called for extensive public education in an area that had both district and at-large candidates running at the same time. The women demonstrated a degree of political skill most professional politicians had not thought possible.

In Illinois, the ERA faced a number of obstacles. As the ERA was first being discussed, the legislature decided that approval of a constitutional amendment would require a three-fifths majority, rather than the simple majority required in the past. In addition, other issues, besides the ERA, have influenced the voting. In 1978, for example, five Democratic representatives from Chicago refused to vote on any legislation before the Illinois General Assembly until an intra-party conflict over the manner of choosing in-party leaders was resolved. The ERA was brought to the floor while this issue of leadership was still being fought. It received a majority of votes but was short of the three-fifths majority required for passage.

After the defeats and the experience in state legislatures, proponents of the amendment agreed they faced two general challenges in addition to the need for political skill. First, they had to reach out to homemakers in an honest effort to understand their situation, and to make these women a visible part of the movement. Second, they needed to educate themselves about their opponents—their philosophy, goals, interests, organizations and funding. Both these needs were already recognized and the experiences of 1975, in particular, provided impetus for moving on them.

The bridge building to homemakers is an on-going and reasonably successful activity. In some instances all that has been needed has been to make visible and to explain the on-going activities on the agenda of local organizations.

The study of the opposition is also a continuing effort. To date, advocates of women's rights have learned that those who oppose the ERA and other aspects of the women's movement agenda can be placed in one of two groups. The majority of opponents are men and women who see the society changing and the viability of its institutions eroding. They are especially worried about what is happening to families—about the economic pressures families face, the fragmentation of family life, and the rise in abortions. At the same time they see women taking on new roles, roles that sometimes challenge their ideas about men and women. Many of these people are church people and often explain their views on women and family life in terms of religious concepts. With no overall analysis explaining the pressure they feel in terms of major shifts in the economic and social systems, these people suspect the women's movement may well be the cause of the disquiet and unrest in our society. They also recognize, however, that some of the claims made by the movement are valid; women, for example, do have many gifts and skills. Many feel that women should receive equal pay for equal work and should not be discriminated against at work. They are left with ambiguous feelings. Although distrustful of the movement, they are aware that it carries some truth.

There is another group of people who recognize in the women's movement and the Equal Rights Amendment a real threat to their interests. These are people who gain significant economic, political, and/or social benefits from the present inequality between men and women and other inequalities in our society. They are represented by such groups as the John Birch Society, the Ku Klux Klan, The Conservative Caucus, The Eagle Forum and STOP E.R.A. Some, such as the KKK, have been on the scene for a long time and are clearly recognized. Others such as The Conservative Caucus are a part of the New Right, an emerging collection of organizations and individuals that believe now is the time to cut back efforts to further democratize our nation.

The ERA is not the only threat they see, however. These people and the right-wing political groups they form view society as composed of 1) small groups of people who have the moral and intellectual ability to direct the society and 2) the great mass of people who should meekly follow directives from above. They act to limit and if possible reduce people's participation in the decisions that shape their lives. Little is said about the fact that the stratification of society they advocate supports a corresponding economic stratification, maybe because they tend to benefit from it.

Right-wing political groups praise and give verbal support to such essential human institutions as local communities, neighborhoods, religion, and especially the family. However, the policies, especially the economic policies, members practice in the long run undermine these same institutions. Their opposition to workers organizing in labor unions, for example, undermines the financial security of many families. Their decision not to provide mortgage and home improvement money to neighborhoods, redlining, leads to their deterioration.

This group also links international politics to the domestic scene in an invalid manner. They see the world divided basically into two camps: the United States and the Soviet Union. Any criticism or questioning of the United States policy or practice is seen as undermining the U.S. With this perspective they tend to see any person or groups that wish to modify the status quo even if only to reduce contradictions between our ideals and behavior as communist or communist-inspired.

For people of this ultra-right-wing ideology, the ERA represents one more effort to break down existing social structures. At one stroke it would give a whole group of people, who have been labeled less capable and dependent, legal equality with those who have dominated our society. To prevent this the John Birch Society, the KKK, The Conservative Caucus and other groups, as well as individuals such as Joseph Coors of Coors Beer fame, have contributed substantial funds to anti-ERA efforts. These organizations have also supplied personnel for the campaign and funded some STOP E.R.A. leaders. It is worth noting in passing that many individuals involved in this network earn their living in businesses such as the insurance industry, which will have to change practices if the ERA is passed.

Extension

When the seven-year period for ERA ratification came to a close and the amendment was still three states short of final approval, proponents decided to seek an extension of the time for ratification. On October 7, 1978 Congress passed legislation extending the deadline to June 30, 1982. The extension is unique in U.S. constitutional history and probably will be tested in the courts before the ERA finally becomes law. Two points especially raised questions: the legality of the extension itself and the question of recision.

The struggle over extension made clear the amount and intensity of feelings stimulated by the Equal Rights Amendment. Proponents and opponents alike conducted campaigns aimed at Congress, the media, and the public. In the end, Congress after consultation with the Justice Department believed it had the right to vote an extension. Legislators arguing for extension pointed out that in many instances the amendment had not been considered on its merits. In addition, they noted that many constitutional amendments had been passed on to the states with no time limit and that the time limit was a recent practice based on convenience and efficiency, not on legal principle. They also made clear that the time statement was a separate piece of legislation, not a part of the amendment itself, and like any other legislation could be changed. Even so, because the ERA extension was the first such action many argued against it on the grounds of legal precedent and wisdom. Also, a substantial number of opponents of the amendment felt that the rules were changed just when they believed they had won.

At the time the ERA extension was voted, three states, Nebraska, Tennessee, and Idaho, had passed resolutions rescinding their approval of the Equal Rights Amendment. During the extension debate, efforts were made to combine extension with recognition of the recisions. The efforts failed. In the past when questions about the legality of one or another activity carried out during the ratification have come up, the courts have left the decision to Congress. Congress did not recognize the recisions of ratification of the 14th Amendment, the only other instance when that occurred. However, as the question of the extension itself, recision will, in all probability, be tested in the courts before the ERA becomes effective.

Which Future?

Whether to ratify the Equal Rights Amendment or not is only one of the many difficult decisions facing us as a nation over the next few years. The ERA may not seem as momentous an issue as the energy crisis or inflation. Nevertheless, how we respond to the challenges of the future will be strongly influenced by whether or not we have an ERA. Without it women will continue to be treated as second-class citizens, and their insights and needs will be given low priority. Some women will be able to develop their gifts and skills and contribute to the national well-being. But these women will represent only a small portion of the talent available to us.

If the ERA is passed by June 30, 1982, there will be a two-year period in which to bring both state and federal laws into conformity. As noted above much of the rewriting will be straightforward but some will be difficult, requiring that we bring together conflicting, strongly felt views.

This will also be a time for us, the people, to get a little more used to living with equality. It will give us time to find out how different people deal with the difficulties, confusions, and awkwardnesses that arise when an idea becomes an actuality. For many of us the changes will be slight. For some it will be a continuation of an already adopted life style only now with more approval. Some of us will have to grapple with conflicting ideas and values. It will not be easy. The deep-seated attitudes of individuals will not change as easily as the wording of our laws. But there will be some surprising satisfactions involved.

The process, of course, will not end there. Court cases will refine the interpretation of individual laws and in the process contribute to our understanding of what equality for women and men means.

If the ERA is not ratified by June 30, 1982, progress on achieving equality for women will continue. However, it will be a slow, costly process. Costly not only in terms of money and time but costly in terms of pain and frustration for women, costly in terms of human resources left undeveloped. All indications are that those favoring the ERA are ready to begin the process again if necessary. Therefore, the ERA will not, as some politicians have hoped, just go away.

Undoubtedly, if another round should be necessary, it will be different from this effort in some significant ways. Money will still be scarce; however, women's political know-how and skill will have developed substantially. The number of women who see the need for an Equal Rights Amendment keeps growing. The defeat of the ERA at this time can only increase those numbers. If we don't see to it that American women and men are equal before the law, now, our children and grandchildren will be left with the need not only to enact an ERA but to undo all the damage that will occur because we have not had one.

It's been a long time since Alice Paul wrote the Equal Rights Amendment, about 60 years. Our society has changed substantially since then. Where once the ERA represented a questionable vision of a few independent women, it is now the goal of millions of women. We cannot afford any longer the cost in injustice and waste of human gifts and skills that is a part of treating women, half of us, as children, as legally inferior. It will not be easy learning to live with an ERA. There are risks involved. We will make mistakes. But the biggest mistake would be to let this opportunity to build a more just, more human society pass.

Suggested Readings

Barbara A. Brown, Thomas I. Emerson, Gail Falk and Anne E. Freedman, "The Equal Rights Amendment: A Constitutional Basis for Equal Rights of Women," *The Yale Law Review* (Vol. 80, No. 5, April 1971).
An indepth study of the legal history and ramifications of the ERA from the perspective of the amendment's supporters which has become a basic reference.

"The Continuing Controversy Over the Women's Equal Rights Amendment," *Congressional Digest,* June-July, 1977 (Vol. 56, No. 6-7).
An overview of the debate about the ERA including statements pro and con by recognized spokespersons.

The National Commission on the Observance of International Women's Year, *The Legal Status of Homemakers [name of state],* (available from the Superintendent of Documents, Government Printing Office, Washington, D.C., 20402, at a cost of $1.25 each).
These booklets, prepared in 1977, spell out in layperson's terms the actual legal status of women with regard to marriage, property rights, credit, divorce and widowhood. (Information or changes in state law can be obtained from state commissions on the status of women in those states where they exist.)

Wisconsin Governor's Commission on the Status of Women, *Real Women Real Lives: Marriage, Divorce, Widowhood* (30 West Mifflin Street, Madison, Wisconsin 53703).
Although some of the legal information applies only in Wisconsin, this is an excellent resource book on women's rights which includes stories of women, answers to common questions and suggestions for further resources.

4.
A GLOBAL MOVEMENT

There is probably not a nation in the world where people are not grappling with questions related to the changing situation of women. In the past few years, Italian women have taken to the streets in pre-election demonstrations demanding changes in divorce and abortion laws. *The New York Times* had reported that one event that triggered the Afghani resistance to the Marxist government, resistance that led to the Russian invasion in 1980, was the government literacy campaign directed at women and other efforts to involve women in activities outside the home. Maureen McTeer, wife of a recent Canadian Prime Minister, Joe Clarke, has kept her own name after marriage, raising apprehensions in some Canadians.

Surprisingly, despite significant differences in cultures and political and economic systems, there are also some themes common to women everywhere. Changes in family structures, roles of women, especially employment-related roles, and relationships between men and women, as well as questions about child-bearing and child-rearing, are issues before societies world-wide. These issues, however, are cloaked in different questions and concerns in different areas of the world.

The sketch of the global dimensions of the women's movement that follows is just that, an outline. Many rich details are lost in the generalization. Significant differences in culture and socio-economic structures are brushed over. Hopefully, however, the discussion will provide a foundation for the wealth of information and insights about women that is becoming available.

PART ONE: WOMEN IN THE DEVELOPED WORLD

Women in Western Europe

Three Lives

Each morning Ingrid Palme, like other suburban women, heads

into Stockholm where she teaches at a technical institute. Her confidence and happiness is obvious as she works with students and shares stories of her two children with colleagues. She sounds like a very modern woman as she explains that her husband Gunther is home caring for the children. If you ask her, however, she will tell you how difficult it was to reach that decision.

Under Swedish law a previously employed parent who stays home caring for an infant or very young child will receive a subsidy to ease the financial burden. The law applies to men as well as women. When her son was born four years ago, Ingrid Palme stayed home with him for two years. Although she loved her baby dearly, she found those years very trying—she missed her job and contact with other people very much. Still neither she nor her husband considered that he take time to care for their son.

When she became pregnant a second time, Ingrid and Gunther talked a lot about the possibility of Gunther being a full-time parent once the baby was three months old. Neither was sure about their decision when they decided to try it. A few friends supported them; their families and most of their friends were skeptical. The first day Ingrid went back to work was, she claims, the longest day of her life. Everytime she heard a phone ring she felt her pulse racing; when the principal stopped her in the hall she expected bad news. That day passed with no problems at home and so did the next, and the next. At the end of a month, when she and Gunther evaluated their experiment they found they had many more good things to say than they had complaints. Gunther found that even though his experiences caused problems, and a lot of the neighbors questioned their wisdom, he was enjoying his new life very much. The children were full of surprises. He was seeing the world through new eyes. And because Ingrid and he had firmly scheduled it, he kept in touch with his work colleagues and spent some time doing the reading and studying he had wanted to do for a long while. Now, nine months later, they have agreed to continue the arrangement for one more year. Then they will both be able to arrange 30-hour-work-week schedules and share parenting more equally.

Maria Costelli is a quiet self-effacing woman, typical of women of the villages of southern Italy. At 30 she looks about 40. At 18 she married a man eight years her senior. Rocco is a good man who has tried without success to improve his family's economic situation. Four of their children are in school although Rocco would rather his oldest child, a girl, find a job. That, though, is the one thing about which Maria has opposed him. She has insisted that Anna stay in school and is now talking about secondary school. Rocco won't hear of that, but Maria keeps encouraging Anna.

If you asked Maria she would say that Rocco is the provider for the family, she's "only a homemaker." If you watched her, however, you might see that she is a provider also.

Maria gets up before anyone else in the household and begins preparing breakfast and other food for the day. She goes behind the small house they live in to a communal tap to get water for cooking and cleaning. Then when the water and breakfast are ready she rouses her family. Rocco and the children leave, she cleans, does laundry in the tub in the yard, and prepares some lunch for the children. In the spring and fall Maria takes the two younger children with her to their plot of land about two kilometers from the village. The food she grows on the plot feeds them a good part of the year. Hauling water a half a kilometer and watering the plants is a time-consuming task. (In summer Maria leaves Anna in charge of the household and goes to the plot early in the day.) She works three to five hours depending on what must be done. On the way home she shops for eggs and pasta. Its time to prepare supper when she gets home. Anna helps if she or the others have no homework; otherwise Anna helps the younger children with their school work. Maria wishes she could supervise the children's school work but she never did learn how to read.

The older boys are free to play if they have no school work but six-year-old Rosalie is responsible for watching the two little children while Maria gets supper ready. When Rocco gets home the meal is served; usually that is at seven o'clock except when Rocco stops with friends at a cafe before coming home. Maria serves the family before eating herself. Sometimes, there isn't much left.

After supper, Rocco joins his friends on the street, while Maria puts the children to bed and sews. The sewing varies, sometimes it's for the family, more often it's for a merchant in the city. Maria is skilled and supplements the family income by her sewing. She knows the merchant gets almost 10 times what he pays her but when she's asked for more money he's said no, that his expenses are high and he can't afford to pay her more. Maria doesn't believe him and would like to see if she could find another buyer. Rocco says no, they need the money and cannot take the chance of switching. He always adds that she should be grateful for what she gets.

Maria would like her two daughters to live differently but she's not sure they can. Rocco doesn't like her to talk "that way."

For Zilla Makal daily life is a frightening puzzle. Even after two years she is afraid to wander off the route that goes from her cramped apartment to the laundry, where she works all day, and to the small shops, where she finds food that is familiar. Her husband

and his friends say it is better for them all to be in this strange, crowded German city (whose name, Aachen, she can hardly say) than for her husband to be here and she and their four children to be in Turkey. She wonders; so do the other Turkish women she meets. Zilla is a migrant. Eight years ago, just after they were married, her husband came here to work. He returned home for a visit every other year and on his last trip he insisted that she and the children come with him.

When Zilla reached Aachen with the children it quickly became clear that she would have to find a job if they were to survive. Friends of her husband told her of the laundry. The work is hard and hot with only 20 minutes at noon for lunch, but there are other Turkish women there. When she gets home on dark, damp evenings she's tired but she must prepare supper and get ready for the next day. Her husband is clearly disappointed in her and the children. He complains about the children's noise, Zilla's poor cooking, and her failure to serve him properly. He drinks alcohol with the other men—an evil forbidden by Muslim law.

The children are also a concern. The two older ones go to a German school. They can speak the language better than Zilla but that is all they seem to be learning. They are not doing well in school, and they are becoming more and more undisciplined. She does not have time to teach them Turkish ways or more importantly about being a Muslim. The two smaller children are cared for by a neighbor but Zilla can see they are not cared for properly. The baby is sickly. She feels frightened and trapped.

At lunch six weeks ago, Lila, another Turkish woman, told Zilla and her friends about a church worker she met. The church worker said they were being cheated, that their pay is lower than the laws allows. Zilla is afraid of this kind of talk. What if the boss hears! They will all be fired. The church worker has invited all the women to stop at a women's center on Saturday, but most of the women haven't gone. Christians, they know, are not to be trusted. But Lila has gone and what she says is almost unbelievable. Someone told them in Turkish about the German food in the stores—how to make it taste good. There are also German lessons, and the children are helped with their school work. Next week there will be a doctor to see young children. Zilla is tempted to take the baby. But the people there are Christians, and Germans, just like those who call cruel words after her as she goes home at night. She cannot decide.

Change and Challenge

The women portrayed above are caught in painful change. Even when they seem self-confident, like Ingrid Palme, they move uncertainly. For migrant women, like Zilla Makal, their insecurity is heightened by language and cultural barriers and a near paralyzing loneliness and isolation.

The situation of European women varies substantially with their class, education, and nationality, yet there are some common issues of concern. Like their U.S. counterparts, European women are trying to give new meaning to traditional values and institutions. They live with old myths and new social realities. Practical rather than legal equality, work, and health care are important concerns.

Equality

The contrast between the myths that govern women's lives and the reality of those lives is sharp. Women have achieved a high degree of legal equality in many countries, yet have found barriers when they try to exercise their rights. Family laws, one test of women's actual equality, vary greatly. In at least half of the countries of Western Europe, including Switzerland, Austria and Ireland, a husband is still regarded as head of the family with control over his wife's finances and other decisions. So far women have not been able to remove the structural barriers that restrict promotions and salaries in the work force. History shows that a very small percentage of women have played important roles in European politics and business but the experiences of these women are atypical and mask the actual situation of the overwhelming majority.

Women at Work

The image of the appropriate role for Western European women is that of homemaker and mother. Yet in most countries women account for at least 30 percent of the work force. In many places, such as Sweden, the United Kingdom, and West Germany, the percentage is higher and the rate of participation continues to increase. As in the United States there are "women's jobs" and "men's jobs." Women's jobs pay less and in some countries, such as Great Britain, include a significant number of part-time positions. This division of work is one reason why, despite laws providing for equal pay for equal work, women's salaries are low. Throughout Southern Europe and in the Asian immigrant communities of Great Britain, substantial numbers of women are employed as at-home workers doing piece work such as sewing. As elsewhere, the pay is very low. Once women dominate a particular work area, whether it be a skill or profession, the area loses status.

All indications point to an increase in the number of women in the work force. Calculations show that for European families living in towns, it is less economical for women to stay home and run households than to go out to work and buy services and ready made products. This is true even if the women have no particular job-related skills; running the household includes sewing, knitting, preserving, and making food from scratch as well as all mending and house working. The only exceptions to this new situation are those rare families with a large number of children.

Although inflation rates in most parts of Europe are less than in the United States, it is still a problem and compels women to work for pay. Better education and different job opportunities motivate younger women to look upon work outside the home as a lifetime activity. In Southern Europe, for example, where women have traditionally married younger than their northern counterparts, women are postponing marriage in order to have a career. The majority of men as well as older women are not pleased with this behavior.

Health

Concern about health has brought women together in many parts of Western Europe. The concern is broad, including general health care and health care delivery systems, as well as pregnancy, childbirth, contraception, and abortion. Over the past four years local groups that have raised health issues have formed networks for sharing information and support. These networks have been particularly effective in spreading information related to the safeness of drugs. The Boston Women's Health Book Collective, authors of *Our Bodies, Ourselves,* and similar U.S. groups, are often members of these networks.

Generally the women of Europe place the abortion issue within the context of health care. Abortion is legal in most Western European countries, however, the evidence indicates that legal abortions are not readily available. The debate over abortions has often been angry and polarizing and is far from over in most instances. The debate has also included arguments that have received little general hearing in the United States. Many of those advocating passage of a law permitting abortion in Italy, for example, identified abortion as violence. They argued that legalized abortion was a historical necessity because of the very large number of illegal abortions. At the same time, they strongly urged actions such as sex education which calls attention to the sexual responsibility of men as well as women, the end of violence against women, and more attention to the needs of women. These actions, those arguing for the legalization of abortion asserted, will make abortions unnecessary.

The Women's Movement

The women's movement in Europe differs from that in the U.S. in some important ways. The movement in each European nation is shaped by the national environment and history. The impact of class on the society and the women's movement is substantial. For these reasons and others the movement seems to be made up largely of local groups, such as the Belfast Women's Collective, which puts out a bi-monthly newsletter, *Vindicacion Feminista* of Barcelona, Spain, which publishes a magazine, the group that runs a women's cafe *Frauenzimmer* in Basel, Switzerland. As mentioned above, these groups often form networks to explore common interests and share information and strategies for action. In addition to health care, networks have formed around the issues of rape and violence against women.

Socialism in theory and practice has been important to the movement. The more activist groups such as the Redstockings in Copenhagen and the more successful political actions have involved women who identify themselves as socialists or socialist feminists. Socialist theory and to some extent practice has promoted equality of the sexes as a necessary element in creating an egalitarian society. Nevertheless, sexism is common and the groups that spring from a socialist foundation are strong in their critique of socialism's failings.

The social security/social welfare base of most European societies is substantial. As a consequence many of the rights and benefits U.S. women have been seeking have been achieved in Europe. Paid maternity leave is common and in some nations women have job protection for one or two years after the birth of a child. Child care facilities are not sufficient to meet all needs but they are available. In France, for example, nursery schools are free and 86 percent of all three-year-olds attend.

The Western European component of the women's movement is international in its outlook. Geography and history both foster cooperation across national boundaries. The international perspective often extends beyond Europe to Africa and other parts of the Third World, reflecting already established networks and economic ties. The International Feminist Network, for example, is a Geneva-based network organized to mobilize worldwide support for women whose human rights are being denied or abused.

Issues for the Future

Western European women are going to have to build their future out of some very contradictory elements. The advent of a consumer society has led to a decline in the economic value of household work. Even though all the services and benefits women bring to their family as full-time homemakers cannot be reduced to economic categories. This lessening of the economic value of homemaking raises questions for the future. Inflation will cause women to consider working outside the home. Better education for women will have the same effect.

Working outside the home does not look very attractive when factors are considered. Women's jobs are low-paying with limited opportunities for advancement in most instances. Women are more vulnerable to unemployment than men and unemployment is rising in many Western European nations.

Until now, most women have derived their status from homemaking and child-rearing. Furthermore, traditional values, in effect, sanctioned the double-day of work and household responsibilities for women who are in the work force. Men have not had household responsibilities. These traditions are now being questioned but they still strongly influence women's ideas about themselves and what they can and should do.

Cultural values are supported by religious values. Christian religions, which have formed Western European culture, have defined women as wives and mothers. Thus, women who question the viability of traditional roles in today's society are challenging religious values as well. Even so, there is much evidence that women and men alike are questioning traditions. Families are smaller; younger women are not leaving the work force once they marry; and the women's movement is growing.

Women in Eastern Europe

Equality in Theory

The situation of women in Eastern Europe tells us much about the rootedness of sexism in Western culture, possibly even human culture. Marxist theory, to oversimplify, has held that with the end of capitalism and class conflict, discrimination against women would end. Sexism, it is argued, is rooted in the unjust relationship between the owners of the means of production and workers who are the real producers. Once this relationship is ended, once the producers are the owners, sexism, as well as class exploitation, will end.

The women in the socialist societies of Eastern Europe, however, have not seen the end of sexism. In the last few years there has been some public discussion of the special burdens of women and a growing awareness of the need for change. How much of that change has actually taken place is hard to say. Information about these women is not easily accessible. This is especially true of the kind of information that gives a feel for the day-to-day lives of people. Any picture drawn from the material that is available is, of necessity, incomplete and probably distorted. Still, some generalization can be made.

Helga Budweiser faces the contradictions, common to women in Eastern European societies, daily. Married, the mother of two young children, she works as a journalist for a suburban Prague weekly. The socialist ideal of creating a just society captivated her long ago. As a student, she took extra courses in socialist thought. Even now, she is well-read on the topic. Despite her strong attachment to socialism, she is convinced it has serious flaws; scholars and practitioners have not analyzed sexism. The burdens of that value grow; heavier each year.

One of Helga's responsibilities is to interview workers who meet production quotas or otherwise merit public commendation. She interviews few women. Over the past two years she has talked with many of the other workers in the places she visits. She has made a special effort to talk to women. They are usually shy when they begin to talk to her but if Helga is patient they will talk about their problems. Concentrated in low-paying jobs, women receive fewer promotions and little recognition. Most complain about being tired and not having time; few of the married women mention any help from their husbands at home. They all report that the services they keep being promised, laundries, cooked-food shops, and child-care centers, are not yet available. Their complaints are Helga's own.

Helga has been married for seven years. She feels it is a good marriage. Jan now does some household chores and he takes the children out a few hours on Saturday afternoon when the weather is good. He is more helpful than most husbands, but Helga still feels she works a double day.

The Budweiser's are in the midst of making a major decision: should they, or should they not have a third child. Jan would like another child. Pointing to all the government incentives, Jan argues that they can afford a third child. Helga has doubts. She does not think that she can care for a third child and continue to work. Few women have. Without her pay check she feels that they could not even afford their two children. It is not that she does not like children or has some ideological objection to a third child, she keeps telling Jan. But how, she asks, are they going to manage? In her snatched minutes of quiet, Helga finds herself debating the question. They are a relatively well off family, yet their apartment is too small now and money is tight. If only the system did match all the theory. What should they do?

Women in the Work Force

Throughout Eastern Europe women are well represented in the work force. They account for over half the work force in the Soviet Union and the German Democratic Republic, and from 40-45 percent of the work force in most countries. Women are found in a great variety of positions: farmers, heavy industrial workers, doctors, and scientists. Discrimination against women in the work place is legally prohibited. In addition, women have a variety of pregnancy related benefits and protections. Women in Hungary, for example, receive five to six months fully paid maternity leave and may claim a child-care grant until the child is three. The latter allows a woman to remain at home with her child, provides her with some income during that time, and assures her of a job when she is ready to return to work.

Despite laws and socialist theory, however, women face inequities. Women are found in just about every type of work but they are concentrated in low-status, lower-paying positions. Some of the discrimination they face is hidden—for example, slow promotions. As maternity benefits and relief time for children are extended, women encounter more difficulty in finding work. Managers prefer to avoid the inconveniences of providing benefits for women and hire men instead.

When women come to dominate a profession or area previously seen as men's, that field tends to lose status. Seventy-five percent of the medical doctors in the USSR are women, and general medicine no longer carries with it high status or high pay. Furthermore, leadership and other prestigious positions are occupied mostly by men. Seventy-two percent of all secondary school teachers are women yet few achieve key positions. Sixty to seventy percent of all farms in Poland are managed by women, because men work in industry or other non-agricultural areas. Women must work the farms, manage their households, and care for the children, without many of the services taken for granted in cities and towns. For this almost impossible set of responsibilities women receive little return, not even increased public acknowledgement of their important contributions to societal well-being.

The Double Day

Most women work full-time on the job then leave to take up their full load of household chores in nations where labor-saving goods and services are just now becoming widely available. A recent report from the Soviet Union notes that women spend an average of two hours a day shopping and then rush home to spend up to six hours on cooking and household chores. Husbands rarely help out in this work.

Ideas held by men and by women about roles do not include men helping at home. A 1977 Soviet magazine article tells of a farmer in Baltic Latvia who is at home during much of the winter. He helps out with cooking and cleaning then. Yet his wife does not talk about his help because she is afraid of being condemned by friends and neighbors. A recent survey in Leningrad indicates that only about three percent of men help with shopping, one of the more time-consuming tasks Soviet women face. Another study indicates that in Poland's major cities husbands and children help with the household work in only about five percent of the families. Many women also face the added pressure of their husbands' displeasure with their being in the work force. A 1976 study in Poland, where 70 percent of the women between the ages of 20 and 54 are in the work force, showed that about two-thirds of the men wanted their wives to be at home. For most men, it seems, a wife's work is accepted as a necessary evil.

Reproduction

Birth control and abortion are legally sanctioned throughout Eastern Europe and there is every indication that both are widespread. Birth rates for example are only slightly higher than in the United States and abortion rates equal or surpass those in the U.S., despite government policies that favor an increased birth rate. Pregnancy allowances and child-care provisions have been adopted with the goal of promoting child-bearing. The Yugoslav government states in its law that abortions are out of date and harmful, yet has little success in reducing the abortion rate. Other nations are beginning to restrict abortions.

A woman's right to responsible control over her own reproduction has been a long-standing part of Marxist and other socialist theory. In most instances, the introduction of family planning and abortion services did not generate very much public debate. In some countries illegal abortions have been a traditional, if unacknowledged, method of birth control. In others, such as Poland, religious and social traditions strongly condemned abortion. However, even in Poland which has the lowest abortion rate in Eastern Europe, about one-fifth to one-third of all pregnancies end in abortion. The scarcity of birth control services and contraceptives is one important reason for the high abortion rates. The need for women in the work force and two incomes to support a family, women's double burden of job and housework, and the scarcity of housing help explain this low birth rate.

The Heritage of the Past

To understand some of the contradictions faced by women in Eastern Europe today it's important to recall the pre-World War II society and World War II itself. Industrialization was well underway in Eastern Europe prior to 1939. Cities like Budapest were as modern as any other in Europe. Yet the nations as a whole were peasant societies heavily influenced by tradition. Roles for men and women were clearly defined. Economics as well as tradition supported women's role as homemaker and mother, and women from their childhood were taught to serve men.

These traditions die hard. Attitudes, especially those related to relationships linking men and women, do not automatically change even if the economic structures of the society do. Socialist leaders seemed to believe they do and thus have ignored the need to confront sexism. As a consequence, women have new opportunities and responsibilities and the old ones still remain.

World War II has also influenced women's lives. The war wrecked havoc in Eastern Europe. Twenty million Russians died in World War II, almost six million Poles (including 3.2 million Polish Jews), and 1.5 million Yugoslavs of which 1.2 million were civilian. More died in the harsh years following the war. One consequence of this destruction of lives has been an imbalance between the number of men and women. In the Soviet Union today, for example, women account for 53.9 percent of the population, men 46.1 percent; there are only 547 men over the age of 44 for every 1,000 women. This is a partial explanation of the variety of work opportunities for women. If women didn't do the work it wouldn't be done. After the war, Eastern European nations faced first the need to recover, then to catch up with the West. Soviet occupation and policies designed to promote Soviet growth caused severe hardships for the other nations in the Eastern bloc. This, too, placed burdens on women. Again, if people were to survive, women had to contribute in new ways to the society.

Tradition, and the impact of World War II plus the anti-dissent policies of Eastern European governments have meant that feminism is difficult to find in Eastern Europe. The many women's organizations that exist are important for meeting local needs and for motivating women in the work place, but they have not served to generate a feminist consciousness. In the past, women from Eastern Europe who have attended international meetings have never mentioned the double burden of job and home life that they and their sisters carry. When questioned, they have dismissed as inconsequential the discrepancies between governmental claims and the actual experiences of women that outsiders have observed.

Over the past few years there has been a change. Experts have traced problems like high divorce rates, slow population growth rates, and even some inefficiencies in the economic system to the unfair burdens women carry. Public reporting and discussion of these findings are underway. Governments have talked of responding. More consumer goods, particularly those which will meet women's needs, are becoming available. Services, such as prepared-food stores, are being reorganized so that working women can take advantage of them. Whether goals will be met, whether women's burdens will be lightened, remains to be seen.

It also remains to be seen if the effort to promote women's rights now found throughout the world will take hold in Eastern Europe. Since marxist and other socialist traditions in theory support equal rights for women, it should. Reports from China, Viet Nam, and Cuba tell us that, to date at least, a real effort has been made to improve the situation of women. Many stories of the Soviet Union just after the revolution included examples of efforts to improve women's lives. Recently an underground publication, a *samizdat,* called *Almanakh: Women and Russia* surfaced in West Germany. It was an anthology containing poetry, stories, and reports about men's drinking and also child-care centers where food was so scarce workers used their own money to feed the children. There are reports that the women who produced the *samizdat* have been threatened with arrest if additional issues are published. The fact that the *samizdat* was produced indicates that some Russian women are willing to speak out for women's rights. One cannot help but wonder just what would happen to women and the whole of Eastern European society if the elimination of sexism were to become a priority in Russia and in the other states.

PART TWO:
WOMEN IN THE DEVELOPING WORLD

Africa, Asia and Latin America: Similarities Despite Differences

The ways in which the lives of women in the developing nations differ are legion. Culture, physical environment, and political and economic systems vary between and within nations. On the more personal level, there are diverse styles of married life, responsibilities, and opportunities for education, work, and self-direction. Despite the mind-boggling differences, the women of the Third World share some common concerns and face similar problems. Customarily they are looked upon solely as child-bearers and servers. They are the poorest, denied opportunities for education and employment. They have little or no leisure, are often hungry, and have little if any control over their own lives. Yet they hope for a better life for their children. They appreciate the wholeness of life and cherish its small pleasures.

The lives of women throughout the Third World are shaped by efforts for economic development. This process of 1) increasing the nation's economic base, 2) improving people's lives and, 3) strengthening the nations' economic and military security is the first item on the agenda of every Third World nation. Yet for some women especially, development has often meant an increase of burdens and a loss of status.

Ketut Martajo knows about development, and she isn't sure it is a good thing. When she hears from her sister Tri in Jakarta she is even less sure about its benefits. Ketut lives with her husband Djumadi and their three children in a village which is a two-hour bus ride from the city of Bandung in Java. Djumadi owns two acres of land, which meet the family's rice needs, with a little extra for the market in Bandung. They started growing chickens last year and earned a little more money selling eggs. Still, they need more cash; they must pay higher taxes on their land and services for which they once bartered rice, must now be paid for with cash. For the past two years the Martajos have worked as day laborers on larger farms during the harvest season. They were fortunate to find that work but it is exhausting and means they neglect their own fields. Their rice yield would improve if they had more water and fertilizer but their farm is too small to be connected into the irrigation system that the government with the help of the Americans is building. They cannot afford to buy more fertilizer.

Ketut feels she's a blessed woman even though her day begins before dawn and ends long after dark with no free time. In addition to cooking, housekeeping, and caring for the children, Ketut works about six hours in the field each day. She also makes two trips to the stream half a mile away for water. In all of this, she is no different from the other village women. Her marriage, however, is different from that of many others. Djumadi makes no family decision without talking them over with Ketut. He has said that he wants a small healthy family and they have agreed that four children would be just right. There are rumors that a literacy team will come to the village and much to Ketut's delight, Djumadi has urged her to try to attend.

When Ketut thinks about how well Djumadi treats her she wishes her sister Tri would come home and marry. Tri went to Jakarta four years ago to earn money to help her parents. She works in a factory assembling electronic parts for computers using a microscope. She is supposed to work 10 hours a day, five-and-a-half days a week but usually she must work an additional 10 hours overtime each week. She is relatively well paid, $1.05 a day. This leaves her with 15¢ a day after she pays for food and rent. She sends her parents about $2.50 a month.

When she came home last year Tri told Ketut about the promises for better pay her employer has made but failed to keep and about the women who were fined for being late two days in a week. She also complained about the liquid that burns her hands, smells that make her choke, and the microscope that gives her headaches. Tri would like to find a different job but the few other jobs available pay less. Tri's vision has begun to blur and that frightens her, for if she cannot see clearly she will lose her job.

Ketut is sad for her sister, for Tri's future holds few promises. For herself, Ketut knows that she and Djumadi will always be close to poverty, but, if they can hold onto their land, she believes they will have a good and happy life.

Development

Development is a complex process that enables the people of a nation to have a human even if minimum standard of living. It is the process in which the nation mobilizes its resources to provide food, shelter, education, employment, and medical care so that the people are not hungry and do not live lives of unending misery. The West has served as the model, but it has proved to be an inadequate model. In the West the process of development took place over centuries. Time and a richness of resources meant that the injustices of one period could be ameliorated in another. History shows that until recently production of goods and services lagged behind needs, but usually not too far behind. There were wars and conflicts during the process but they did not engulf the whole world.

The situation for Third World nations and peoples are different from those of the developed world. Communications, especially with radios and films, make the world a small place and there is pressure for rapid development. People who are hungry in India know there is an abundance of food in the U.S. Poor parents worried about an ill child in Brazil know that medicine is available to those with money or those who live in the right places. The pressure for change is greater than many governments or societies can cope with. The eradication of epidemic disease, some public health measures, and improved nutrition has meant that more people, especially children, live longer than in the past. This, for example, puts demands on the food and educational systems that they cannot meet. New technology changes the way things are done, creating some but not enough new jobs. Industrialization seems the answer but the cost, in both money and social upheaval, is high. Global politics creates a sense of insecurity in every nation. Even developing nations spend a significant part of their foreign exchange for new weapons.

Women's Heritage

Women are caught in the vortex where traditional society and development efforts confront each other. In most Third World societies, the traditional division of labor based on gender has limited the opportunities of women. These limitations are reinforced by a belief that women are inferior; a belief held by women and men alike. Women throughout the Third World express the wish that they were men! They tell of hearing their fathers wish that they were boys. A Buddhist woman in Sri Lanka told an American writer that she had been born a woman because "she had sinned a thousand times in a previous life." New laws that give civil and economic rights to women are ignored because they are a major break with tradition.

There was a balance in traditional societies that softened the harshness of life for many women. The social restraints also placed burdens and responsibilities on men, although, except for the most poor, these seem to have been far less onerous. Supports for women, like the extended family, were built into the social system. Child care was usually shared. Women could gain status and respect for doing their traditional jobs well.

Women, Food, and Hunger

A woman in Africa might tell the story of the impact of development by going back to the time of her great grandparents when land was held in common by the extended family. Men prepared the land, women did the actual farming. If the weather conditions were favorable there was enough food. Colonial administrators changed this land-holding system: it could not be taxed easily. They required that the land be registered in the names

97

of individuals, men. In time, the need for cash to pay taxes and buy necessities, once obtained by barter, and the dream of a better life led men to migrate to the cities and mines. The women, left behind in the villages with the full responsibilities for the children and old people, did the best they could. Then came the development effort, one part of which was the improved agricultural production.

Western experts focused their attention on men, who they assumed to be the farmers. Their African counterparts, used to overlooking women, did not correct them. Men who had never been farmers received agricultural training. The owners of the land, men, were given access to new seeds, fertilizer, credit, and new tools. Women, the farmers, received no resources. Men began working on plantations and large farms that produced agricultural products for export; coffee, cocoa, cotton, pineapple, and so forth. The women, however, remained responsible for the family food. The "surplus" that many women marketed had become an important source of food for townspeople as well.

The need for more food grew as more children survived infancy, as common diseases no longer killed and as people moved into the towns. But the women farmers were unable to produce enough. Everyone, families and townspeople alike, suffered from hunger. Equally important from the perspective of individual women, they lost status and respect because they were not properly carrying out their traditional task of feeding the fmaily. It was not until 1972-74, during the world food crisis, that experts and some national leaders began to appreciate the actual role women have in food production. Some attempts have been made to make resources available to women but it is very hard to overcome traditional attitudes and practices.

Rural Development

In developing countries most people live in rural areas, so rural development is a major concern. It has two goals 1) to improve the production of food and other agricultural products and 2) to improve the lives of people living in the countryside. Usually the same components—water, food, employment, education, energy, health services, access to markets, credit, and appropriate technology, to name some—serve both goals. Efforts to provide these components have often failed because the critical role of women has been overlooked.

Around the developing world women are the water fetchers. They carry water for home use and in many instances for irrigation. This fact is not usually noted until a scheme has failed. In Nepal, the U.S. Agency for International Development, as a part of a major water develoment program, helped build a three-village water supply system, which was to improve irrigation and bring water for cooking and cleaning. As in the rest of the program, some men from each village were shown how to keep the system, which piped water down a steep mountain repaired. When an AID consultant returned to one of the villages three years later the system was not working because of broken and clogged pipes. It didn't take too long to understand what had happened. Since the men didn't carry the water they had little interest in maintaining the system. The AID consultant was a woman, sensitive to the importance of water to women. She arranged to have women shown how to repair and maintain the pipes: that part of the overall system now works.

The outcome of a World Bank project in Africa did not turn out as well. New wells were dug close to a village to replace some further away. The village women knew the seasonal variation in the water level in the old wells was substantial, but no one consulted them, and because of custom they could not speak out until asked. The new wells were not dug deep enough and the women must still travel more than five miles to get water during the hottest part of the year.

Sometimes efforts to increase production are very successful yet are harmful to women. Poor women have earned food for their families in Indonesia and India by harvesting the rice. This contribution to their families is essential. Recently cutting and milling machines run by crews of men have both replaced women and spurred production. The former workers do not have the money to benefit from the increased production. No one has suggested that this new technology should not have been introduced. But, those concerned about the welfare of the poor have asked why the needs of women harvesters weren't recognized and some alternative employment provided.

Industrialization: A Twisted Dream

Industrialization has been a goal of many national development plans. Throughout all of the developing world industrialization and its promise of jobs has stimulated urbanization. Poor families seeking work and a better life have moved to cities only to find little work and harsh living conditions. Some eventually acquire skills and break the cycle of poverty, more do not. For women, urban living brings problems without solutions. They are far from their family and usual support system. Urban living means living in a cash economy but women, without skills, find it difficult to earn. Crowded living conditions increased health and sanitation problems.

Although women are generally excluded from industrial jobs, there are exceptions, especially in the textiles and electronics industries that export to the developed world. For women, this industrial employment is a mixed blessing. It provides them with much needed earnings but often at a high cost. The women are generally underpaid, even from that perspective of the local cost of living. They work long hours under close supervision and poor working conditions. Each type of industry brings unique problems. Women in the electronics assembly plants found throughout East Asia, work using microscopes. At 25 or 26 their eyesight is ruined and they lose their jobs. The dust in textile factories causes brown-lung and other diseases. No matter what the industry, production demands are high, leaving women exhausted each day and physically worn out while still in their 20s. The sweat shops that we in the U.S. have tried to eliminate are being rebuilt in Asia.

Two factors have militated against the women organizing to change their situation. Women have been trained from childhood on to be docile and meek. They expect hardship. Most fear that if they made any effort to change things they would be quickly labeled troublemakers and fired.

These fears are well justified. Governments in industrialized Asia and Latin America have adopted policies that encourage the exploitation of workers. There is much competition among developing nations for foreign industrial investments. One way to attract companies is to guarantee profits and a passive work force. To do that, governments allow less than subsistence wages and ban labor unions. In Korea, for example, women working in factories that make shirts for the U.S. market have been beaten and otherwise mistreated, even jailed, because they wanted to elect their own representatives to the government controlled union. The fact that they were women, daring to take some control of their own lives, resulted in extra abuse.

Education: Carrier of Hope

Educating women, the common myth held, was both dangerous and wasteful. As a result only a minority of women received any education and just a handful of wealthier women had an opportunity for secondary or university education. Denied education, most Third World women have clung to traditional attitudes, knowledge, and practices. Their illiteracy and inability to understand new ideas has, in turn, been cited as another sign of their inferiority and used to justify further discrimination.

National governments, foreign aid donors and women's groups have worked hard to overcome the education gap. Efforts to keep girls in school have grown. Programs focusing on functional literacy are widespread. Also common are courses designed to train women as health workers. Programs which have impact income-generating skills and crafts are growing. The American Friends Service Committee (AFSC) to cite one example, set up a training program for Malian tie dyers. Women in Mali who had begun to dye fabric, possessed basic skills but needed to learn advanced techniques. AFSC arranged for women from eight development centers to receive training from women in a Gambian dyers cooperative. After learning the new techniques and seeing how the cooperative worked, the Malian women returned home to teach others and set up their own cooperative.

The women trained in these organized programs put their skills to work, and also became teachers and trainers, multiplying skills. It almost goes without saying that the resources available do not meet the needs. Although the number of literate women has grown, the percentage of literate women has dropped as the population had increased. According to the most recent UN statistics, in 1960 women accounted for 58 percent of adult illiterates; in 1970 this number had climbed to 60 percent.

Education and employment were among the topics examined at the United Nations sponsored Conference on Women held in Denmark in July, 1980. The World Plan of Action, prepared at the Mexico City UN International Women's Year Conference in 1975 cited both education and employment for special attention for the following five years. The major purposes of the Denmark conference was to determine the progress in these areas and in women's health, and to strategize for the next five years. Education and employment are not just the concern of governments and elite women. Perdita Huston who recently traveled to six developing nations reported, "Nearly every uneducated woman I encountered—whether she lives in a rural or urban area—expressed a yearning for education." This was true of the young Tunisia woman who peeled labels off cans because she could not afford books and wanted to practice her reading. It was also true of the Mexican Indian woman who answered Ms. Huston's question "almost aggressively" and stated, "I would educate women *more* than men. Women bear and raise the children—so women prepare the future. How can the future be good if women are ignorant?"

Population

Population growth in Third World nations was one of the first issues to cause development experts and government leaders to look closely at the situation of women. The spectrum of approaches to population growth has ranged from looking at women as persons and creating situations where they have an effective voice in deciding family size, to looking at women as things to be manipulated to achieve a goal.

Population growth became a pressing concern for many Third World nations because efforts to improve health, though inadequate, have reduced death rates. The end of epidemic diseases and the survival of infants have been welcomed but have also meant more people. In many countries half or more of the population is under 15 years old. These children make demands that communities and families cannot meet. In rural areas, for example, children help with farming but still, food production may not be high enough to feed them adequately. If these young people are going to contribute in an increasingly complex society (and their societies are evolving), they need education, another cost. The list can be expanded. Aurelis Peccei, president of theClub of Rome, notes that between now and the year 2000, 1,000 million new jobs will be needed, most in the Third World. How are they to be created?

From the perspective of the individual family the answers to questions about family size differ widely. The conditions of a modern technological society are not yet present in developing countries and social mores support large families. For wealthy families with access to good health care, the idea of responsible parenthood is comparable to that of many U.S. parents. Expecting their children to live, couples provide their children with a good education and prepare them for life in a modern society. These families, while often larger than the average U.S. family, are becoming smaller.

Poor families live in a very different reality. They do not expect half their children to live. Because there is no social security system parents look to children to support them in their old age. Thus, it is important to have many children. Planning for all but the most basic education of children seems unrealistic, for even if schools are free, the required clothes and books are expensive. Even at a young age children can add to the family economy by working in the fields, selling newspapers, scavenging, and so forth. (In Bangladesh a boy by age 12 may bring into the family more than it spends on him, and by 22 has earned enough to pay all the costs of raising him and a sister as well.) Finally there are the traditions that measure masculinity and femininity by the number of children a couple have: these too pressure for larger families.

Traditions that define women as childbearers also tend to deny women the health they need to carry out that role. Poor nutrition is common among Third World women for they often eat what is left after everyone else is finished. If food is scarce, women eat little.

Anemia is a major debilitating disease. There are not enough health facilities so that even simple problems are untreated and become major. Finally, in many instances women have no say about how many children they will bear; that decision is the husband's, not a joint one.

The response to rapid population growth varies widely from no response in many African nations, to all out campaigns to reduce family sizes in some Asian states. The strategies advocated also vary. At one end of the spectrum are those that advocate a social justice approach; at the other are those who advocate mass campaigns and penalties for those with more than two or three children. The social justice approach calls for changes in the social environment so that babies will live, and the creation of a social security system so that old people will have economic resources. The approach calls for a fair distribution of the benefits of development, especially health, education, and employment opportunities, so that people can hope and work for a better life. It also calls for changes in attitudes about the roles and worth of women.

Other programs focus only on distributing birth control devices and convincing couples to have few children. The Indian sterilization program, motivated by a crisis situation, fell into this category. In between are programs that include maternal and child health care, education, and birth control services. The churches in the Philippines, for example, have organized centers to teach natural family planning.

One extreme response to population growth, triage, has been advocated by some Western experts. It's advocates argue that the ratio of population to resources in some nations is so bad that the nation should be treated as those who are involved in a disaster and will die no matter how treated. Foreign economic and technical aid only encourage people to reproduce. Therefore all aid, even food aid, should be ended and the people be alowed to manage any way they can, even if it means many deaths. This position is usually argued strongly when food is scarce, such as the time of the 1973-74 food crisis.

Population growth focused attention on women, but, to date, concern for population has not led to meaningful concern for women. Although lip service is given to the need to be respectful of women, population experts more often than not treat them as objects. Officials label them as problems when they bear children—their only access to status in many cultures. This approach to population growth that places women between a rock and a hard place points to the necessity of changing attitudes about women's roles and worth.

Women in Decision-Making

There are very few women in key decision-making positions. Women themselves as well as their concerns and interests suffer because of this. Grassroots women, researchers, and analysts keep running up against the same stone wall: when policy is being set, women's needs and work are not among the factors that shape the decision. As a consequence, policies and programs, especially those designed to reach the poor or promote basic human needs, fail in achieving their goal and also add to women's burdens. Women are often excluded from participation in development projects, and at the same time are denied the resources to carry out their traditional responsibilities, then labeled as barriers to development.

The Plan of Action drawn at the 1975 International Women's Year Conference calls for the *integration* of women into all levels of decision-making at the United Nations and national government. The plan urges that women be placed in decison-making and policy-setting positions throughout the UN and governmental structures. In addition, it recommended the setting up of a commission of women and advisory groups that could effectively voice the concerns of even the poorest women. Regional and national plans of action prepared since 1975 contain similar recommendations. (Most of the resolutions passed at the 1977 First National Women's Conference in Houston have a similar component.)

Globally, the response to this call has been minimal. The reasons vary. For example, in all but a few nations women have been denied the necessary education and experience. In the Third World there is a scarcity of trained people, men as well as women. In societies where women have been considered less capable, it is difficult to convince leaders of the value of preparing women for governmental and corporate responsibilities. Many men and women, insensitive to what is at stake, also see this attention to placing more women in decision-making positions as push for power on the part of the elite women, and therefore ignored it.

The number of situations where women have been integrated into decision-making are so few that it is difficult to back this argument with success stories. Yet there are some. About 35 percent of the professionals and decision-makers of the United Nations Fund for Population Activities are women. Recent programs, respectful of women as persons, have begun to focus on population concerns within the context of wider development questions. One program, for example, has provided training to women so that they can take advantage of new employment opportunities.

The Women in Development Office of the U.S. Agency for International Development (AID) has been doing research that has provided important information about women. For example, the number of households headed by women is higher than anyone thought: up to one-third of all households in parts of the Caribbean and Southern Africa. This office has been holding seminars and other programs designed to make AID officials aware of the many responsibilities of women. The goal is to assist officials prepare programs that will integrate women into development efforts in a way that will benefit women as well as achieve desired goals.

A Perspective on the U.S. Women's Movement

For many Third World women the concerns of women in the U.S. or Western Europe are puzzling. Third World women are not sure they are equal to men. They do not want to do the same work that men do. Their desires are much more closely linked to survival. And yet as their needs and dreams are examined more closely it is apparent that these women, like women elsewhere in the world, are struggling to create a better life for themselves, their families, and their communities.

Third World women present a special challenge to women of the United States when they ask what can women do, what does it mean to be a woman. They look to U.S. women, who have an education, a little more free time, and more material goods for support. First they ask for understanding. Then they ask that we keep them in mind as we make decisions. The policies the U.S. government adopts on trade will impact their job opportunities. The decisions of U.S. transnational corporations influence the resources their nations have for development—for education, and health facilities, for controlling their own destiny. These corporations, through their employment policies, determine how individual women will live. Third World women ask that U.S. women be aware of that.

The course of the U.S. women's movement, itself, will influence the lives of women and children in developing nations. The movement's many organizations serve as models. The skills U.S. women gain do likewise. The issues U.S. women choose to raise are particularly important to Third World women. If in the end the issues struggled with strengthen family and community the Third World women will be supported in their efforts to create a better life. If not, Third World women will have a harder time gaining recognition of their personhood.

Conclusion: Women Uniting

In recent years we have witnessed an unprecedented examination of the situation and experiences of women. As part of the process, women have begun to share their dreams, concerns, and oppressions. One reason for this interest in women and their lives is the contradiction between the myths that shape women's lives and the lives that they live. A second has been the cost to family and society of stereotyping women and limiting their roles. The need to reassess the place of women in our global society prompted the United Nations to proclaim 1975 International Women's Year (IWY). As part of the year's activities the UN sponsored a World Conference in Mexico City. The IWY and the Conference stimulated research and other activities to promote the well-being and rights of women. A Plan of Action was adopted at the Conference and since then similar plans have been adopted by many nations. The UN Plan calls on governments everywhere to look more closely at women and their lives and also for an International Women's Decade (IWD) to focus efforts to improve the situation of women.

The Conference, the Plans of Action and IWD were important but they would have amounted to little if it were not for the activities of women's groups and individual women. IWY and the World Conference provided an opportunity for women to learn more about each other, their strengths and their needs. It promoted much sharing, the practical, how-to-do kind, and the probing of new ideas and of possible solutions to vexing problems. It has led, as well, to the building of informal communication and support networks.

The meetings and exchanges at and since Mexico City have not been without problems. Women with different experiences and world views have clashed over a range of issues: the definition of women's issues, the value of women-specific development, importance of women's traditional roles, to name just three. Women from industrialized nations have their nations and their socio-economic systems denounced as oppressors. Women from the Third World have been criticized for the ease with which they dismiss the problems facing women of the developed world. Most of the women involved in IWY/IWD activities found that they had much more to learn about women. And most women developed a new appreciation for women's gifts and strengths.

The 1975 IWY Plan of Action recommended a mid-decade conference to evaluate progress and to strategize for the remaining years of the Decade. The World Conference on the United Nations Decade for Women held in Copenhagen in July, 1980, focused on the issues of women's health, education, and employment, and questions of political oppression. The Conference debate centered on government-sponsored actions. But, as in 1975, the Conference served as an occasion for women to come together to share experiences and new knowledge. It also served to strengthen and expand women's networks. The Conference was one more step to integrating women fully and effectively into our global society.

Suggested Readings

Perdita Huston, *Third World Women Speak Out* (Praeger, New York, 1979). A survey of the opinion of women in six countries on issues such as education, health including reproductive health, and family relationships.

Lynne B. Iglitzen and Ruth Ross, ed. *Women in the World* (Clio Press, 1979). A collection of essays on the situation of women globally which includes an examination of women's legal rights and employment opportunities.

Hilda Scott, *Does Socialism Liberate Women* (Beacon Press, Boston, 1974). A very readable study of women in Eastern Europe which concludes that socialism must come to terms with sexism.

ISIS (available from ISIS, Case Postal 301, CH 1227, Carouge, Switzerland). An international quarterly devoted to women's concerns from the perspective of feminist and grassroots organizations.

5.
WOMEN, FAMILY, AND THE WOMEN'S MOVEMENT

Beth and Mickiel van Helmunt sip their tea and agree that the pressures they feel as husband and wife and as parents are different from those faced by their parents. Whether the pressures are greater is another matter for these just about middle-aged parents of four.

Beth is the daughter of Irish immigrants who struggled to make ends meet all of their married life. They provided Beth, her sisters, and brothers with the education they needed to build a materially better life. The cost in long hours of work and scrimping in an unfamilar culture was high. Beth doubts if the pressures were any less than those she and her husband experience.

Mickiel grew up as a middle child in a comfortable, middle-class Dutch family. Yet, his family struggled to maintain a sense of family security in the midst of the turmoil and devastation of World War II.

The van Helmunts sense that family life is declining in value in our society. They cite not only rising divorce rates but many other factors such as materialism and individualism. Inflation and real estate speculation has changed the character of the middle-income child-oriented neighborhood they moved into nine years ago. As families move, usually because of work-related transfers, they are replaced by wealthier, older couples. Their children must look further and further for the playmates their parents sought to provide them with when they chose the neighborhood.

Has the women's movement influenced their life? Yes, both claim. For one thing it has reinforced their belief that they both have home responsibilities. Mickiel spends more time with his four young children than most of the other fathers they know and he also helps out with the housework. The movement has also helped make them more sensitive as they make some decisions. The van Helmunts expect that in the next few years they will reexamine their decision that Beth should be a full-time homemaker. Their reevaluation will include not only family needs and Beth's wishes but a careful look at work opportunities and patterns that are emerging because of pressures generated by the women's

movement. Mickiel feels he is treating his children differently
he would have if there were no women's movement.
encourages his daughter's ball playing as well as his son's cool

The circumstances of her life influenced Beth's judgment o
women's movement. A homemaker for 12 years, Beth notes: "
27 when I married, almost 29 when our son was born. I knew w
was giving up and had a realistic idea of what I was ta
on. I had a chance to gain my own identity and to come to k
what my values really were. This has made it possible for n
respond as a friendly critic to the movement. I think it has ra
some very important issues, and usually it has done a good jo
describing the problems of homemakers, but it hasn't told o
pleasures of being a full-time wife and mother, and I don't a
with many of the remedies that it has encouraged."

Beth sees parenting as a demanding, at times drain
responsibility, yet one with many rewards. Until the last year or
she feels that the women's movement rarely mentioned
rewards. She wonders aloud if women, even those who are
sympathetic to the movement, appreciate the many
homemakers have. In the past she felt the movement certainl
not. Until recently, it seemed to her as if movement women ta
of choice while conveying the message that homemaking
really not a choice of a reasonable woman.

In the last few years there has been a change, Beth th
Women speak more appreciatively of the importance of h
making. Increasingly, she feels, there is some mutual su
among homemakers and the women's movement activists.

The van Helmunt's experiences with the changing rol
women and men and their evaluation of the women's move
represent only one set of responses. It reflects, in part, their
than average marriage age and their family backgrounds.
sets of experiences lead to other judgments.

The Langos and Martins are no more typical than th
Helmunts but they too reveal much about our society and the
of the women's movement within it.

Like the van Helmunts, Anna and Joe Lango have been m
13 years. But Anna and Joe were just 21 when they married
dreams included more education, careers for both, and a
They are achieving those dreams but not the financial secur
took for granted. They have always had work but bec
changes in both the economy and employment opportuni
jobs have been temporary positions.

Economic security is not the only pressure they feel. I
they both work outside the home, they find themselves fac
needs and problems not faced by their parents or relative

care has been one major concern. Although the quality of the care offered has been their first consideration, they have also had to be attentive to cost. They have been, in the end, usually satisfied with the arrangements they make, but they feel as if they use a disproportionate amount of their energy in the process. They also find that they constantly question and reevaluate their priorities. Anna has had to learn to live with a less ordered home if she is to spend time with Joe and their two children. Even though Joe shares child care and household tasks both he and Anna feel they have little time for just being together or for their individual interests. They realize now that there is a dimension to their decisions that they are just beginning to appreciate. Each decision seems to involve a choice between old roles and new. Both find that no matter how reasonable the decision is they continue to question it from the perspective of what they "ought" to be doing. Without minimizing Joe's feelings, Anna believes that she has the more difficult time: "Women have been trained so well to feel responsible for everything that happens in the family."

In the past Anna held part-time jobs just so she might have more time for the family. She has found herself shunted into dead-end positions with a workload very heavy in proportion to the time. "Full-time work for part-time pay" is her judgment. Now she is enjoying her work in a large hospital but she is often frustrated by working conditions. Those who draw up time schedules do not take into consideration that she and others have family responsibilities. A group of family people have discovered that with a little mutual cooperation they can rearrange their schedules to satisfy both hospital and home demands. They've been meeting regularly for a year; sometimes the administration accepts their revisions, at other times it doesn't—no explanations are given.

Often the Langos feel isolated. They've had to move five times during their married life. Each time it has been harder to find others who share their values and interests. They miss the extended families they grew up with and are saddened because their children have only snatches of that experience.

Their latest move into an integrated neighborhood in a city far from "home" has been a surprise. They have received support and encouragement from two unexpected sources: their church community and some neighbors. For the first time in years the Langos find that the worship services and the activities of their church are addressing some of the questions they face day-to-day. Weekly church services are no longer viewed as an obligation or habit but a real source of encouragement and hope.

Two neighbors have also made a difference. The Johnsons and Smiths seemed to know just how to help: offering to care for the children, sharing tools or a hand, or calling for a coffee break just

when things seemed impossible. They are strong, happy families where both spouses work outside the home—models the Langos appreciate.

The Johnsons and Smiths are black. As they helped the Langos settle in, they made them aware of how the experiences and culture of black families have strengthened their family life. There is little question about Margaret Johnson and Delores Smith working. All four adults come from families where married women have had to be part of the job force to insure family survival. Both families feel very much a part of a large extended family, and the adults work at maintaining and building that feeling. The Langos have learned from both families and value their friendship.

The Langos look very positively upon the women's movement. They have found support for their vision of family life among people involved in the movement. They have benefited by the attention to child-care needs generated by women's organizations. They both believe that work time will be more flexible in the future thanks to women's agitation. Anna thinks that the movement is now dealing with basic issues. She believes, however, that it needs to be more sensitive to the traditions and experiences of ethnic communities and poorer women, and it needs to be more realistic in its approaches to family life. Maturity, she hopes, will help with that.

Sarah Martin admits that the women's movement has been a powerful influence in her life. "It gave me the confidence I needed to make some hard decisions. Some women who were a part of the movement helped me explore the opportunities open to me and also supported me when the going got rough. However," she insists, "the women's movement was not the cause of my divorce." Pete Martin disagrees. From his perspective, the women's movement is to blame for the end of his 24-year marriage.

The Martins married in 1953, after Pete came back from Korea and Sarah finished her second year of college. Except for their large family, their life was similar to that of many other upwardly mobile couples. Pete took advantage of the GI Bill to complete his education. Sarah worked until the first baby arrived.

After earning a M.A., Pete accepted a series of jobs that combined promotions with moves around the country. In 1966 they settled in a university-dominated mid-Western suburb. Their family of seven grew to nine as the tensions that ended their marriage became clear.

They agree on the outline of the next ten years of their life but disagreed on what actually happened. Sarah, with Pete's encouragement, became involved with a variety of university-related activities, including the anti-war and later the Women's Movement. The new ideas and attitudes she encountered challenged her, and, she felt, enriched the whole family. Pete felt differently. He found it especially difficult to accept some of Sarah's thinking about the need to change relationships between women and men and the roles of women. In time they found they could not easily talk about their differences. Their whole relationship suffered.

In 1975, three years after Sarah decided to finish her education, the Martins agreed to a trial separation. They also agreed that Sarah was the one who most needed the space and quiet that living alone would provide. Their differences in values and life styles became even clearer during the time of separation, thus no one was surprised in 1977 when they divorced. Pete retained legal custody of their three minor children while they continued what was in effect joint custody.

Friends, who cared for both, feel that the Women's Movement was key to the divorce, not because it caused the Martins' basic problems but because it enabled Sarah to explore alternatives to the status quo. They think that without the movement, Sarah would have become a bitter, carping woman but she would not have agreed to a divorce. What were the problems? Friends note that for the first 15 years of their marriage, Pete was growing and changing. In addition his wishes determined where and how the family lived. Sarah, for whom marriage was very different from her expectation, had to accommodate. When she objected to one of Pete's decisions or raised questions about their own relationship, Pete did not take them seriously. With their final move Pete was ready to settle down; he wanted no more big changes in his life. Sarah, gaining some freedom from household demands, began to grow and change. Pete was unable or unwilling to change to accommodate the changes Sarah sought; Sarah in turn was no longer willing to compromise her aspirations to accommodate Pete. The Women's Movement made it possible for Sarah to agree on divorce rather than live in a household of continual conflict.

The Family: Is It in Trouble?

Seventy-six percent of the respondents in a survey conducted in *Better Homes and Gardens* magazine in 1977 felt that the American family is in trouble. Respondents attributed the difficulties to inattentive parents, lack of a religious/spiritual foundation, materialism, financial pressures, and divorce among other causes. Fifteen percent of those under 35 compared with 26 percent of those over 55 felt that women working outside the home was a factor.

Better Homes and Gardens readers are not the only people

concerned about the pressures and difficulties facing families. Over the past four years a variety of groups and individuals have looked again at the American family and voiced concern. Divorce, fragmentation of the family, the increase in single-parent families, problems involving children, including crime and drug abuse, and the apparent increased violence in the family are all signs that families are in trouble. Inflation, inadequate housing, poor schools, and lack of facilities for the care of the aged and those unable to care for themselves are problems shared by families and communities.

Urie Bronfenbrenner, a leading child-development expert, believes that Americans no longer value or support the family. He is greatly disturbed by this finding. Others, such as Kenneth Keniston and the Carnegie Council on Children find Bronfenbrenner overly pessimistic but agree that families face serious difficulties. Groups as diverse as the White House, the National Council of Catholic Bishops, and the NOW Legal Defense and Education Fund are responding to this growing concern. They and others have planned programs which they hope will strengthen families and develop new strategies for family life.

As pointed out in Chapter 1, the context in which families live has changed markedly over the past hundred years. The rate of change has accelerated since World War II. The primary causes of the changes have been industrialization and its multiple consequences for our society and for people's lives. Industrialization has separated home and workplace. The family is no longer a production unit. A variety of consequences follow.

The Family Economy and its Culture

The appliances and other consumer goods that have relieved the drudgery and shortened the time of household tasks are a part of industrialization's impact on the household. For all the complaints, few of us would want to get rid of most of them. While recognizing that they are mixed blessings—the washing machine that means clean clothes with little effort also means laundry is done three or four times a week—we feel that the blessings usually exceed the costs.

The industrialization of the household economy has also meant that it is usually less expensive to buy goods and some services than it is to prepare them at home. In practical terms this means that the value of some of the work of homemakers has decreased. This is one factor in the loss of esteem that homemakers have experienced. Another factor which cannot be underrated is that the economic values of homemaking has never been acknowledged. The household economy has never been taken into account when a nation calculates the worth of all its goods and services, its Gross National Product, GNP. If a woman prepares food in a factory or restaurant or cares for children in a day-care center it becomes economically valuable. If she does these same tasks at home they have no monetary value and are considered to have no economic value.

Children are also an economic cost in an industrial society. In pre-industrial agricultural societies such as found in the U.S. before World War I or in Third World nations today, children contribute economically to family well-being. But in the United States, today, children are a financial liability, rather than an asset. It is important to insist that the worth of a child cannot be reduced to dollars. Nevertheless, children are a large expense. Education and medical care add to the cost of feeding, clothing, and housing a child. One 1977 report estimated that it cost at least $35,000 in direct costs to care for a city child until he or she was 18. Inflation raises that figure every year. Responsible parenthood means that couples must take this cost into account as they create their family.

Because children are expensive and basic necessities such as housing are also high, many women are forced to seek employment outside the home. The Labor Department has estimated that an urban family of four needed an income of $11,546 in 1978 to achieve a "lower-level" standards of living. The contributions of over 60 percent of the married women in the workforce raised the family income to this level. Many more employed women raised family income to the "moderate" standard of living level, $19,000 in 1978.

Continuing inflation means that more women will have to join the work force if families' current standard of living is to be maintained. Even then, many families may be forced to change their living style.

The need for women to seek employment has been accompanied by a demand for women in the work force. Employment, especially in those fields traditionally considered women's work, such as clerical and health care, has expanded significantly in recent years. Skilled and experienced workers in these fields are actively sought. Thus many women have found that when they considered rejoining the work force there was a place for them.

Other factors also encourage women to seek work outside the home. It is less expensive to buy many household goods and services than to prepare them at home. This has contributed to a decrease in the status attached to homemaking at a time when money has grown in prestige. More often than we may care to admit, a person's income has become a significant part of our regard for that person. The growth of individualism has meant that the husband's professional achievements no longer guarantees the wife the same status. This two-fold loss of status becomes concrete when women without careers find in both civil and social settings that their ideas and comments are ignored. The wife of a teacher and the wife of a clerk are expected to know little except how to please their husbands and raise children—and sometimes the latter is questioned. The prestige that a job would bring becomes very attractive.

Homemaking in the 20th Century has also meant isolation from the larger society. Loneliness and a lack of intellectual stimulation are important causes of the depression many mothers of young children experience. Women used to the intellectual exchanges of school and work keenly feels its loss. They describe themselves as stagnating and begin to lose their self-confidence. A job, almost any job, would end this isolation for many women. The problems accompanying the decision to go back to work, especially when that decision is reinforced by economic considerations, seem more manageable than the isolation and lack of esteem many women experience as homemakers.

When a wife and mother becomes a part of the work force marriages and families face difficulties. One set is common to all women who work outside the home, whether they are middle class, working class, poor, minority, single parents or even single women without nuclear family responsibilities. Time for family and friends, household tasks, time for church, community, even political affairs, and time for self become challenges or problems. Childcare is a special concern. All these difficulties become challenges when a woman finds the support she needs; problems when support and services are not forthcoming. Lack of leisure, the double duty of home and job, and child care ranked among the top four problems cited by 110,000 working women in a fall 1978 survey conducted by the National Council on Working Women. Inadequate pay ranked number one.

These difficulties are widely recognized and are receiving attention from a variety of groups and organizations. The fact that they are clearly recognized as problems is in itself an advantage. It helps couples, single parents too, realize that the difficulties are not theirs alone. It also means that people are seeking solutions. Suggestions like shifting the structure of work for pay by allowing flexible time schedules, for example, or shorter work weeks with a fair share of benefits, including access to promotions, will not solve all these problems but they will help. The size of the female work force means that some of these changes will be made. The passage of an Equal Rights Amendment will mean that men as well as women will benefit, for the changes won will be available to men, too.

There is a second set of problems facing couples, especially middle-class and working-class couples, when wives enter the work force. They stem from each's expectation of what marriage and parenting mean and their willingness to change themselves and their attitudes as the marriage progresses. How severe these tensions are, and how they are handled, often determine if the marriage will survive. Much depends upon a husband's attitude and reactions.

Many husbands feel guilty when their wives enter the work force. They expect to meet the financial needs of the family and hold themselves responsible when they don't. A great deal of pride may be involved in this expectation. Often, men fail to acknowledge that changes in economic structures have had a significant role in their situation.

Some husbands resent their wives joining the work force because it disrupts their lives. They expect that if they carry the financial burden of the family, their wives should make no other demands on them and should respond to their every need. For some of these men, children may be resented because they demand attention. When their wives work outside the home, even for pressing financial reasons, these men expect that their home life will not be disrupted. When it is, trouble follows.

Finally, some husbands become very jealous. They distrust their wives and the attention they may be receiving from colleagues. This too creates burdens that their marriage may not be able to bear.

When married women join the work force they change. Their priorities may shift: a neat, clean house may become less important especially if it is solely the wife's responsibility. In many instances, a woman's self-confidence and self-esteem grow. Not only does earning her own money give her a feeling of independence but it holds a promise of rewards for work well done in the form of promotions and a higher salary.

The strength of the relationship and the degree of agreement about a wife's decision to return to work are just two elements that determine how a couple manage the tensions that accompany a wife's entry into the job market. How hard they work at building their marriage is another. In a large number of cases one or another, or both spouses, are unable or unwilling to make the necessary adjustments. Sometimes the communications within the marriage have been poor and cannot be rebuilt, even though the need is great. In instances like this, the marriage breaks down completely. Today most damaged marriages end in a divorce.

In most instances when a wife becomes a part of the work force, couples continue to build their marriage and family life under a new set of conditions. Their struggle makes clear that we are in a time of transition. Many times they feel they're exploring new territory. They are frightened and fearful of the mistakes they might make. They do not have many models they can follow. Often their best efforts are frustrated by things they cannot control: inflation, needlessly inflexible work structures, a failure on the part of employers to give more than lip service to the needs of family life.

The influx of women into the work force has had its effect on the women who remain full-time homemakers. Their families, too, find their lives changed. The homemaker becomes more isolated while experiencing more demands on her time and energy. There are fewer women who share her day-to-day experiences and concerns. It is not unusual for one woman to be alone on a block from nine in the morning until the children get home from school. Neighbors, even friends, may not have the time to share interests; some even put down homemaking. New friendships are hard to build. A busy husband is not able to provide all the essential companionship.

The women at home are also left with the responsibility for a growing portion of community service. Schools, churches, and other services that depend upon volunteers have a decreasing pool of people to draw upon. Women with children in school, for example, find themselves in constant demand as room mothers, cookie bakers, and trip sponsors. Some always respond cheerfully, others, at peace with their own set of priorities, respond when they can. Some, believing the myth that they should be available when called, feel guilty when they must say no, while still others, resentful of the demands and angry at the women who are not there, respond grudgingly. When homemakers cannot respond to these community needs, they must be paid for or left unmet. Increasingly it is the latter. Organizations find themselves with dues paying members but not with persons to carry out programs. Children's activities, such as Boy Scout meetings, once held in the afternoon are now scheduled for the evening or not held at all. Even when a mother is not part of the work force, family life must be rearranged.

There are other ways in which the full-time homemaker's life is influenced by the increased participation of women in the work force. For example, her child-care responsibilities increase. Because there are fewer adults in home during the day she must keep close watch on her own children. She can no longer expect that when her growing children join friends after school that a watchful adult will be present. She must constantly determine the fine line between hobbling her children's self-reliance and wisely setting limits. In addition, this same homemaker often finds herself an unpaid babysitter. Her home or yard becomes the gathering place for neighborhood children whom she must regularly supervise. For some women this is no burden, for others it is. In either case it is often unrecognized and unappreciated.

The Family as Emotional Haven

In the past the family was the basic unit of production and procreation. Today the procreation role remains but in place of its production role the family has taken on an expanded nurturing responsibility. It is responsible for the emotional sustenance, healing, and personal growth of all its members. These are not new concerns, but in the past they were secondary to survival and production. Furthermore, the nuclear family was not expected to carry them out alone. The extended family, the neighborhood, and the larger community all had a part to play. This has all changed.

Today the term extended family often describes the location of the family rather than the physically close network of relatives that previously supported the nuclear family in many unrecognized ways. Mobility with its potential for improved economic well-being and personal enrichment has usually removed the nuclear family from its ethic and spiritual roots. Sixty percent of the respondents in the *Better Homes and Gardens* survey cited above believed that mobility has harmed the American family. The more educated the respondents, usually the more mobile, the more likely they were to hold this view. The extended family generated its own set of pressures and tensions, yet it was an important source of support.

Mobility, the evaluation of houses primarily in economic terms, government policies, and societal values have all changed the neighborhood. No longer is it a place of mutual support, shared activities, and pressure to observe societal conventions. People come and go; friendships do not have much time to develop. Government policies and the end of locally responsive small businesses have lessened the control those living in a neighborhood have over it. There are few community recreation areas where people may gather. In practice, "privacy" and "minding one's business" come to mean non-involvement. Not only have the social pressures that neighbors used to bring to bear on each other ended but the safety value they provided has also ended. Often there is no one to take a restless child from a too busy mother or to share a cup of coffee or a beer with an upset parent.

The ties of a family with relatives and neighbors have weakened at a time when they are vital. The process of industrialization has caused changes that have made the society at large less human, more competitive and impersonal. More and more, the nuclear family came to be seen as the refuge from this harsh social environment so that today it is exclusively responsible for mutual emotional support and personal growth. There is an often denied but nonetheless real expectation that husband and wife will meet not only all of each other's emotional and psychic needs but also many of those of their children as well.

This expectation is unrealistic. Furthermore, it is undermined by the contradictory sets of values needed for success in economic life and family life. The society esteems individuality, personal initiatives, and achievement. The ability to go-it-alone and compete are looked upon with great favor. Family life, in contrast, requires cooperation, self-sacrifices, and empowering others. Sharing is essential to building a common future. It is possible, of course, for these two sets of values to co-exist provided each occurs in moderation. At present in most Western societies, this is not the case.

The stress on the emotional content of marriage has led to another question, "Whose marriage?" Jessie Bernard, other sociologists of family life, and researchers like Gail Sheehy have found that men and women have very different sets of experiences in a marriage. Men tend to receive the support and service they look for. Women are less likely to.

For men, home and marriage has represented the opportunity for renewal. Home is where their physical and emotional needs have been satisfied in order to ready them for the "real" world. Husbands could legitimately make demands on their wives and expect they would be fulfilled.

For women the situation has been different. The assumption has been that they receive their satisfactions principally from serving others. Only a word of appreciation, keeping a wife aware of the importance of her service, was needed. Little thought has been given to women's needs for growth or intellectual stimulation, not easily available when one acts only as servant. Some women did have the freedom to be involved outside the home; more did not.

As emotional satisfaction within marriage has grown in importance, these two sets of experiences have been set in opposition to each other. Women have the same needs for self-esteem, actualization, affection, and renewal that men have. Many women expected that these needs would be fulfilled in a satisfactory sex life, an unrealistic burden for sexual intimacy. When this did not take place they blamed themselves and/or their husbands. But blaming alone does change an unsatisfactory situation.

When marriage does not measure up to expectations, couples face a crisis. It is more than the crisis experienced when each realizes the other is not the person he or she was thought to be when they married. When marriage itself does not fulfill one's needs there usually is nowhere else to turn.

How couples respond to an unsatisfactory marriage varies. Many work at it. They talk and share, and eventually form a marriage that satisfies them both. Others reach an accommodation—the benefits outweigh the costs and they live with it. The costs may include constant bickering and unrecognized undermining of each other.

Still others cannot manage and the marriage ends.

The women's movement has been a factor in women's response to the emotional exclusivity of marriage. The movement has allowed women to voice their dissatisfactions and it has also served to make women aware of alternatives, including divorce. The movement has also given some women the impetus to choose this option. It has also led to the development of institutions and organizations that have created space for women to change their lives while maintaining and strengthening their marriages. Both husbands and wives have benefited.

The increased importance of marriage's emotional nurturing role raises new questions for couples, for families, and for those who want to support family life. Just as there are few models for families when both spouses work outside the home, so there are few models for couples and families seeking a realistic and enriching level of emotional interdependence in their lives. Couples, families, and the society are grappling with that all too common problem of our day: how to maintain and strengthen what is valuable while coping with change that we barely seem to understand and can't seem to control.

Things We've Not Thought Too Much About

Education, longer life, smaller families, early marriage also influence the strength of a marriage and of family life. Education and longer life are benefits that have accompanied industrialization. Smaller families and early marriage are characteristic of our late 20th-Century society.

Education has opened new opportunities for men and women. From a glance at other parts of the world, we know that women lose status and benefits if the gap in education between men and women is great. As a society we appreciate the value of education. We have encouraged people in their quest for education in many ways, including better pay and recognition.

In the past, most women have enjoyed the fruits of their education in limited ways—personal enrichment, family enrichment—sometimes as volunteers or as club women. Today, education and the desire to use it is a reason so many women want to combine marriage, a family, and work outside the home. Often as we examine the challenges facing marriages we ignore this. Yet there is a pressing need to create forms of family life that build upon women's education.

A stroll through a graveyard dating from the turn of the century would quickly supply us with one explanation why in the past there were fewer divorces. For many people, life was shorter. The average lifespan in 1900 was less than 50 years; in 1930 it was just 60. Marriages rarely lasted 40 years. There was always the chance that an unhappy marriage wouldn't last too long.

Today the average life expectancy in the U.S. is 73 years. Marriages, not interrupted by divorce, may last 40 or 50 years. During that time both spouses grow and change. Their needs shift. We have always suspected that adulthood was not an undifferentiated span between adolescence and old age. Today, as more people live to become old, we are looking more closely at both adulthood and old age. We're learning more about the complexities of these two periods and at the same time gaining an appreciation of the capabilities of older people for living a full life.

Like so many other experiences, longevity challenges marriages in new ways. Can we build marriages that are strong yet are flexible enough to change as spouses age? Can we build structures that support couples as they pass through different phases of their lives? So far we have only partially succeeded. Marriages end because they cannot make the transitions. Some survive as models of what most don't want marriage to be. Some grow and blossom amidst the problems. We need to know more about these marriages.

Families are smaller today than they were even 20 years ago. The average family today includes nearly two children. Twenty years ago it included almost four children. A small family, even without the added features of early childbearing and long life, would change the responsibilities of women from what they were in the past. Most women who are primarily homemakers end the active phase of their careers as mothers during their 40s. Often they or their spouses had not considered what they are to do with the remaining years of their lives. Men, too, are making career adjustments during their 40s—coming face-to-face with limits or, for a smaller number, dealing with greater responsibilities. As spouses try to adjust to these changes they make demands on each other that cannot be met unless they are understood. Lacking this understanding, many men and women become absorbed in their separate lives and grow apart.

The age at which people enter marriage in the United States is rising. Yet the average age is still lower than that in many other industrialized nations. Many young Americans marry while still in their teens: about 25 percent of all young women under 20 are married. Statistics and experience show that a high percentage of marriages involving teenagers end in divorce: probably over half of them. These young people often marry for the wrong reasons and are unrealistic in their expectations of marriage. T.V. and film romanticize marriage. Their parents may also convey false images of marriage.

Schools and organizations do have programs they hope will

provide the education about marriage that young people need. Pre-marital programs run by churches have the same goal. However, much more thoughtful attention needs to be given to marriage preparation.

The array of issues we must consider as we attempt to support marriage and family life in the late 20th Century is formidable. Yet couples do marry and stay married. Families grow in love, even when marriages do end. The networks of relatives and loved ones survive despite odds. Families are still signs of hope in a complex, troubled world.

The Role of the Women's Movement

Critics claim that the women's movement is anti-marriage and anti-family. The movement they assert plays down the value of family and the traditional role of women by encouraging women to take jobs outside the home. This assessment is false. It is industrialization and the culture it has generated that has destabilized the traditional family. The women's movement is only a response to the problems that already exist. It is important that we be clear about this distinction, otherwise our efforts to create a society supportive of family will fail.

The women's movement has provided a context in which women have identified and focused on some of the problem areas of their lives. It has challenged some assumptions of our industrial society by comparing ideals with experiences. It has made many women and men aware of problems new to our society, problems we might otherwise not deal with. Most important, the movement has suggested some creative solutions to these problems.

Raising Questions, Challenging Assumptions

Which is the better approach: 1) to identify and focus attention on problems in a society before they become acute—and thereby risk the possibility that others, who did not see the problem before, will join in the complaints; or 2) to ignore problems until they are very serious? Are the people who identify problems bearers of negative attitudes or enlightened leaders—or neither? Our answers to these questions tell how we shall judge the relationship between the women's movement and the present change in marriage and family life.

In probing the lives of women, in raising questions about their expectations, experiences, and feelings, the women's movement encouraged women to look more closely at their lives. Marriage is the most significant single event in the life of the majority of women. Family life is a major focus of most women's lives after marriage. It is not surprising, then, that the women's movement has directed a substantial amount of its attention to women and marriage and family.

At the beginning, the movement encouraged a popularizing of the data on hand and the gathering of new information. The movement helped make known the material that scholars of family life had been gathering for many years. Jessie Bernard's *The Future of Marriage,* for example, was published in 1972 and drew upon data going back to the 1930s. However favorable these studies were toward marriage, they tended to show that women invested more emotional energy as well as other resources in marriage and gained fewer benefits than men. The movement also encouraged women to speak out about their own experiences, providing new insights into women's lives. Betty Friedan's *The Feminine Mystique* (1963) served as a model. The studies and the sharing of experiences made clear that many women were dissatisfied with their situations. Both these activities encouraged women who seemed content, to reexamine their lives and raise new questions.

This look at marriage and family was coupled with attention to the benefits of work outside the home and encouraged women to join the work force. At the same time, feminists and scholars were examining other aspects of women's lives. They found much to criticize. Psychologists' definitions of a healthy adult matched that of a healthy male, rather than some combinations of male and female characteristics. Schools operated on the basis of sterotypic ideas of men and women.

The beginning of the movement was a time of discontent, anger, and blame. Women had not yet undertaken the critical analysis necessary to understand the causes of the discrimination they faced. Those who joined the movement blamed men in general and those they knew in particular for their powerlessness and dependency. Everyday tensions between husbands and wives were intensified. The present polarization of women stems from this period as those who were happy in traditional roles felt themselves under attack.

It followed naturally, then, that most assumptions women and men held about marriage and family would be explored by the movement's thinkers. Relationships between men and women, ideas of marriage, and concepts of family life were again questioned. Hardly a value was left unchallenged. Another set of questions sought to explore the relationship between gender and personality. What does it mean to be feminine? Masculine? How much of what we think of as masculine and feminine is actually the product of culture?

These questions did not come just from the women's movement, however. The counter-culture movements of the 1960s raised some of these same questions. The "pill" and other birth control techniques facilitated the sexual revolution which also called into question values and all past sexual wisdom. Commentators and scholars examining American life called our attention to heretofore unnoticed changes that were taking place within the society. Although the number of couples living together without marriage almost doubled in 1970 and 1977, for example, the increase started earlier. The divorce rate in the United States has been growing since 1960.

The women's movement did not have answers to all of the questions raised but at times it seemed otherwise. Some members who had access to a public forum sounded as if their newly formed ideas about relationships between women and men were norms for the future. Others found their questions, their thinking out-loud, and their private lives reported as the latest feminist dogma. Some women tried to put into practice the ideas being developed; most were sincerely seeking a way of living within a changing society.

At first, most people dismissed the emerging ideas as distortions of society's sustaining values. Then slowly, both women and men began to think about the issues being raised. Their thinking was influenced by two factors legitimized by the women's movement: the validity of women's feelings and the recognition that women could lead independent lives.

The personal sharing of that has been an integral part of the movement and has led many women to accept as legitimate, feelings they once suppressed or dismissed. Their feelings of dissatisfaction, their ambitions, their desire for self-fulfillment are now considered worthy of attention. The new willingness of women to respond to their feelings has meant change for spouses and children, as well. The resulting family tensions have either been resolved by mutual adjustments or have created serious problems for the marriage. Without the women's movement, there would have been no effort for change in many cases.

Experience in the work force, by the women's movement, has renewed many women's self-confidence and sense of independence. This self-assurance in turn has enabled many women to make demands on their families and especially their husbands that they would not have made otherwise. Again, the consequences have varied from better marriages and family life to the break-up of the marriage and a radical change in the life style of the family.

Probing More Deeply

As the women's movement has matured, its members have been probing more deeply into the issues first raised in anger. Movement members are more aware of the links between the injustice women face and the societal structures. They recognize that individuals do not so much wish women evil as they wish to maintain their current life style. There is a greater appreciation of the difficulties involved in change and a willingness to respond with encouragement to persons making a sincere effort at being fair. Equally important, there is in the process careful separating of basic values from the structures that support them and of persons from structural roles.

Women and some men, for example, are looking again at the idea of patriarchy and how deeply it is a part of our thinking and structures. Many question how useful patriarchal structures are in our present-day society while at the same time noting how strongly it influences our attitudes and structures. Efforts to deal with patriarchy in marriage are hard, just because they are so deeply rooted in our psyche and society.

Patriarchy is linked to ideas of power: who holds it and how it is to be shared. It is difficult to think of power in the context of that most intimate relationship, marriage, yet it is vital that we do. Their earnings and self-confidence enable working women to make new demands on their marriage. Younger women, used to controlling their own lives, will be less willing than their mothers and aunts to accept their husband's decisions. The need to understand power and how we use it, particularly with respect to decision-making about money and family responsibilities is crucial. By raising this issue, the women's movement is contributing to building more equitable relationships.

Questions about sexuality and value—love, fidelity, intimacy, and so forth—come not just from the women's movement. The movement has encouraged exploration of female sexuality. Feminists, psychiatrists, and physicians have debunked many common ideas about women's sexual responses. The new attention to female sexuality has intimidated some men, creating another source of tension between couples. It has also contributed to the challenging of commonly held sexual norms. This challenging, however, is as much a product of the secularization of our society as it is of the women's movement. The consequences of all this questioning has been varied, even contradictory. Because of the focus on sexuality and sexual behavior we have come to know ourselves better, and to appreciate the many ways our sexuality influences our lives. At the same time many values that have shaped the relationship between men and women and contributed to family life have been undermined. New ideas about sexuality and how it is best integrated into our lives have also generated opposition and fear among the holders of traditional values.

The process of sorting and separating is far from over, yet, the women's movement has begun to understand and appreciate the values it once rejected. As women separate patriarchy from marriage, for example, some who once thought otherwise recognize the value of fidelity and commitment within marriage. Women who formerly considered childrearing an unfair burden, now appreciate the pleasures and satisfactions it can bring.

This renewed appreciation of traditional values is not simply a return to the past. The values have reemerged and are now being lived out in a different way. Thus, for example, a marriage of two persons who have questioned and probed may be built not only on an appreciation of fidelity and self-sacrifice but also on a commitment to equality and empowerment. In practice this may mean that decisions are made slowly, or that far more attention is given to a wife's wishes than has been common in the past.

Some Movement Contributions to Family Life

The women's movement does not have answers to all the questions it has helped raise, but it does have some suggestions of where the answers may be found.

To begin with, many movement-involved women insist that the society in which we live harms men as well as women. Although men have more acceptable options in their lives than women, many feel that men, too, must conform to standards that require them to deny a part of themselves. Thus, the new ways of living out marriage and the new styles of family life will have to foster whole women and whole men.

The women's movement has experimented with shared leaderships, with empowering its members, with processes that keep its members sensitive to all aspects of jobs that must be done, including the drudgery. Women have learned from these efforts; they know some of the pitfalls, and the effort required for success when decision-making is shared. What they've learned can contribute to new patterns of family life.

The movement has fostered a new respect for the things women have traditionally done—nurturing and the domestic arts. Women are calculating the economic values of their tasks. A T.V. commentator recently calculated that a homemaker caring for two pre-school children made yearly contributions worth $35,000 to her family (calculation included pay for on-call time as well as actual work time). Although such calculations are dismissed by some as silly and others as contributing to the disruption of the family, this type of information makes clear the values of homemaking in terms understood in today's society. For some women, this fosters that added measure of self-esteem that enables them to start building a new style of family life.

The women's movement has done a good job in helping women articulate the dissatisfactions and problems they face within marriage and family life today. It has helped make clear many of the contradictions between our myths about marriage and the actual experiences of women.

The movement has insisted that women are equal as persons to men, and that this equality should be recognized in practice as well as theory. In claiming that equality should be lived out in marriage and family life the movement has added to the tensions and problems currently faced by couples and families. At the same time the women's movement has begun to create spaces where women have experimented with new ways to make decisions, and share power and responsibilities. Their experiences suggest that equality and marriage are not opposed; that family life can encompass whole, confident women as well as dependent women.

The women's movement, in challenging the situation of women in marriage and family life has helped us see how our present societal structures have undermined both. In grappling with the issues that the movement has made visible, we have come to realize the need to change many structures in our society. That need would have been present without the women's movement. The movement has encouraged us to act now.

What of the Future?

Our own experiences tell us how important family is to human happiness. Opinion polls show that most Americans agree with that judgment. Moreover, almost all poll respondents, 94 percent, feel that their families are doing at least fairly well. On the other hand, we have many indications that families are facing serious problems. The U.S. divorce rate is high—in 1979 one in three marriages ended in divorce. Given the opportunity, couples voice many concerns. Not only must they struggle with the ever-present tensions that result when two adults try to share their lives but they must also deal with individualism, inflation, inadequate support structures, as well as changing roles. How are families to respond?

The dream of returning to past models of marriage and family life is appealing. It includes the fantasy of a less complicated, seemingly changeless society. Our experiences tell us this dream is much more the temptation to avoid responsibility than to manage the problems before us. To return to the past would mean that some families would have the security and pleasures of the old ways but that many more families would face difficulties and problems made worse because the society denied their existence. It would mean we would continue to build economic and social structures that inflate the cost of basic needs and force women and men into roles that deny many of their talents. We would harm families while claiming to support them.

If we cannot return to the past what then? The answer is not yet clear. Neither the women's movement, nor all the family experts, counselors, nor pastors, or even families themselves can tell precisely the style of family life in the future.

There are some things we know, however. There will not be one style of family life but a variety. The style will reflect the different values that stem from our religious and ethnic heritages, and from the ways those traditions have been modified in our industrial society. They will also take into account the fact that more often than in the past marriages break or do not take place yet families exist and thrive.

The assumption that the successful family is self-sufficient and insulated from outside pressures will be recognized for the myth it is. Families have always relied upon others—the extended family, the schools, the neighborhood, the church. When these structures fail to meet needs, families with some money have been able to pay for services; their lack of self-sufficiency has been masked. Poor families have had to rely on community services and have been labeled "in trouble" for the wrong reasons. Now we recognize that all families must call upon resources they do not always have within themselves. One challenge is to assure that each family has these resources available to it in a way that strengthens it.

Among the resources the family relies upon, the neighborhood has a special place. Families flourish where neighbors work together to create an environment that reflects their common values and goals. Such neighborhoods have the services families need—schools, health facilities, locally controlled stores, and recreational areas. More important, they have an atmosphere of trust and cooperation. People know each other and know that together they can control some of the institutions that influence their lives.

Churches can support families in a special way. As neighborhood institutions they can foster cooperation and provide resources. When churches actively participate in neighborhoods, they give an added legitimacy to all activities and further strengthen the neighborhood.

The church is the institution that has traditionally guided people in finding meaning in their lives. In the United States today we are facing a crisis of meaning. The church alone cannot overcome that crisis for it is not only a personal crisis but one that involves all our institutions. Nevertheless, the church has a special role to play. In dialogue with all its members, and especially families, the church can contribute much to the search for meaning and can renew itself as an effective support.

The women's movement has made clear that one of its goals is to promote a more human society. One component of that goal is the freeing of men to take their rightful place in family and community life. The movement cannot achieve this goal alone. Two ideas now being discussed, the shorter work week and simpler life styles, have great potential for giving family members more time and benefiting all of society.

Time is almost always a concern for families today. The lack of time for anything but the most pressing activities leads to frustration as well as unmet needs. A reduction in the work week would give people the time they need for family and community activities. It would also create more jobs when unemployment rates are rising. Women have been pioneering in creating new approaches to work over the past few years; shared jobs and part-time work with benefits, as well as "flexitime," are no longer rarities. A shorter work week would benefit families and communities, as well as women.

The second common complaint from U.S. families is about money—the lack of it. Inflation is increasing that burden. The Carnegie Council on Children in its recent study, *All Our Children: The American Family Under Pressure* cites money as a key factor in a family's well-being. For low-income families, there is no substitute for more money. For other families, however, there is an alternative, a simpler life style. We have been described, quite accurately, as a consumer society. The evidence is growing that we cannot continue as we have in the past. Resources are growing scarce. Consumption is feeding inflation. And, many of us are no happier despite our many goods.

A simpler life style would not only conserve diminishing resources, it would also help families deal with these two vexing problems of money and time. The cost of living could actually be reduced, relieving the family of some pressure. For some families this might mean that family members could reduce their work time. Homemakers can share in the freeing of time. Kenneth Galbraith in his study, *Economics and the Public Purpose*, points out that a significant portion of the middle-class and upper-class home-maker's time is devoted to managing family consumption. Galbraith's point is that homemakers contribute far more than society acknowledges to the national economy. But he is also pointing to ways families can reduce economic costs and some uses of time.

Creating a simpler life style is a family task. It requires dialogue, listening, a willingness to question most of our assumptions, and a setting of new priorities—difficult tasks made more difficult when we are giving up things. Families will choose different ways to simplify their lives. In some instances it will lead to a greater sharing of household tasks. It most instances, families will find themselves stronger and happier.

Women's struggle for equality will also be a part of the family of the future. The equality of husbands and wives will require a change of attitudes on the part of both. New ways of making decisions will be needed. Openness, more attention to communication, and greater trust will be required. Some of our unshaped assumptions about sexual behavior should be examined under a clear, strong light. For example, underneath many discussions about women in the work force there seems to be an assumption that once women are freed of the restraints of the role of homemaker they will become unfaithful, even promiscuous. There also seems to be an assumption that men are always seeking sexual pleasure. These assumptions, so often only alluded to, raise some real questions about our ideas on marriage and human nature, especially women's nature. Yes, there are promiscuous women—and promiscuous men. Sexual harassment is real. However, the majority of men and women are faithful to their spouses. Sex, though a powerful force in human life, can and usually is controlled and coupled with love.

There are other issues that must be faced as we work to strengthen marriage and family life. Experience indicates that if people marry in their middle or late 20s rather than earlier, their marriages have a much better chance of succeeding. Yet puberty occurs at a much earlier age than it did a century ago. How are we to deal with teenage sexuality in a society where so many teens are alienated and confused?

Friendships are a powerful source of growth and fulfillment. Women and men need strong friendships with persons of both sexes. The claim of friendship between a man and a woman especially if either is married to another has been scoffed at. How can we foster friendships that grow but do not lead to sexual intimacy?

The style of marriage and of family life needed for the future will have to meet the challenges posed by our society. The women's movement response to the problems women face today has questioned our ideas about marriage and family life, and some of our most precious values. The movement has also helped women grow in self-confidence and strength. These women are now free to bring their gifts and skills to their effort of creating styles of marriage and family life that will enrich the whole society.

Suggested Readings

Joan Aldous, *Family Careers: Developmental Change in Families* (John Wiley, New York, 1978).
A study of the changes in family roles as family members mature.

Caroline Bird, *The Two-Paycheck Marriage* (Rawson-Wade, 1979, New York).
A study of how women and men are responding to the increased participation of women in the workforce which includes the perceptions of women not in the workforce.

Judith Blake, "The Changing Status of Women in Developed Countries," *Scientific America* (Volume 231, No. 3, 1974).
A survey of the changes that have occurred in the situation of women in industrialized societies.

Kenneth Keniston and the Carnegie Council on Children, *All Our Children: The American Family Under Pressure* (Harcourt Brace Jovanovich, New York, 1977).
A well received examination of the way social structures, especially economic structures influence the family.

6.
WOMEN AND RELIGION

Cherishing Faith Amid Dissent

Faith-filled People

"My faith is a vital part of my life." "My faith gives meaning to the rest of my life." "Prayer and meditation renew me." These phrases sound familiar to Christian women but they could be and are just as easily said by Buddhist, Hindu, Jewish, or Muslim women. Women of every religious belief find and assert that their faith brings hope and strength to their lives. Many also admit that there is another side to their religious experiences—the traditions and practices of their religions contribute to the discrimination against and oppression of women.

The Center of Concern-sponsored consultation on the Impact of World Religions on Women and Development provided an occasion for exploring the ambiguous relationship between women and religion. The 21 women who were among the 28 participants of diverse religious and national backgrounds repeatedly told of the importance of faith in their lives. Faith had helped some achieve an inner freedom that allowed them to grow despite obstacles. Others noted that their personal faith in God brought inner peace despite failure and disappointment. Many reported that "religion is the glue that binds me to a wider community." That community, often the extended family, provides women with physical, cultural, and spiritual supports.

The participants, women and men alike, also recalled those situations where religion burdens women. Conferees felt that all religions' practices and traditions confined women to the roles of wife and mother, ignoring women's many other gifts and talents. More importantly, participants felt that religions reinforced the idea that women were not mature persons.

A Hindu participant observed that Indian women "are brought up to see God through their husbands" and as a consequence, wives see themselves and are treated as their husband's slaves.

Coptic women, we were told, often hear the teaching of a religious leader as "The Bible gave the easiest job to women: obey your husbands; but the hardest job to men: love your wives." A Jewish woman told of the struggle she has had in responding to the call of the Jewish tradition to serve the community. The life style and training required of those called to be religious leaders are incompatible with her obligations as a Jewish woman. Buddhist nuns have much less prestige and freedom than monks, participants noted. Christian women told of the difficulties women face when responding to the call to ministry. All the participants were aware that Catholic women do not have access to the decision-making councils that affect their lives and are denied ordination to the priesthood.

A Painful History

Paralleling this truth that women are faith-filled despite obstacles of discrimination and oppression is another that also calls us to reflection and renewal. Every religious tradition at its beginning affirmed the personhood and dignity of women. As it formed and spread, the new religion freed women from past cultural and social practices that dominated them. In time, however, the same social and cultural practices overpowered the religion's values. Soon women are again suppressed—by the new religion as well as the society.

Usually, the history of women in the religious tradition remains hidden from the people. Recently, however, it has become more available. Rachel Conrad Wahlberg in her small book *Jesus According to Women* asks us to look at some of the episodes in Jesus' life with newly opened eyes. She reminds us, for example, that it was with Martha, the homemaker, that Jesus discussed resurrection (John II; 17-26). In the Jewish society of the first century, women were not supposed to be a part of theological discussions, yet Jesus' conversation with Martha was only one such report in the scriptures.

The long conversation Jesus had with the Samaritan woman at the well was another (John 4: 1-30). The cultural pattern was again ruptured when the women at the tomb were told to announce the Resurrection. This freeing of women ended soon, however. Paul the Apostle, though a man of great theological insight and creativity, was unable to withstand entirely the cultural pressures of his age against public roles for women. Several passages in his letters legitimized the imposition of cultural restraints on women.

This process is not restricted to Christianity. Jewish women ask why the stories of strong, creative women, such as Deborah,

Miriam, and others, stress their role as nurturers at the expense of their roles as prophetesses, poets, or leaders. Such questions are not intended to minimize the importance of women as nurturers but rather to reveal the whole spectrum of women's roles and experiences.

Muslim women have a corresponding history. Scholars who study the *Koran*, the Muslim holy book, cite passage after passage that affirm the equal dignity and responsibilities of women and men. Responsibilities within marriage differ for women and men but they are portrayed as equal in value. The male-dominated culture of the Middle East, however, submerged these teachings of the *Koran*. Women are now segregated, most are illiterate and must rely on others even to tell them about God. Popular religious practices and myths are cited to keep women in inferior positions. Wealthier, educated women are sometimes able to challenge the status quo, but poor uneducated women are trapped in a world of religion-supported subjugation.

The Hindu experience is similar. Somehow, over time, the position of relative freedom and opportunity that Hindu women had in the past has been narrowed. Now women question the evils of their previous life that allowed them to be born as women. The Buddhist experience has been somewhat different. Within Thailand and other Buddhist societies, women manage family finances and property and have a say in village activities. Women have extra responsibilities as wives and mothers, and men are treated with special respect. Yet, women and men have fairly equal responsibilites. Such status must be placed in another context, however. The secular is considered an inferior realm in Buddhist cultures and men seek status and power in the spiritual domain. Within that sphere men are clearly superior in practice. The lives of Buddhist nuns are carefully regulated by traditions and rules that do not apply to men. Buddhist societies are now beginning to secularize. Whether Buddhist women will retain their position in family and society when the secular realm becomes as important as the sacred is an open question.

Confrontation: A Sign of Hope

Against this background the confrontation between women and religious institutions can be interpreted as a sign of the importance women attribute to the spiritual dimension of their lives. If, as some experts claim, women are religious because they are brought up to be so, then we could expect that those women who are disillusioned and angry would turn their backs on spiritual activities. Many do. But significant numbers, while turning from the institutions, keep seeking ways to nourish their spiritual life. Some eventually do find riches within the institutional church where feminism is recognized as a valid spiritual stance. Others seek and grow bitter in their frustration. Georgia Fuller, 1976-1981 chairperson of the NOW Task Force on Religion, reports that she is often called upon to help plan liturgical services to provide information about religious services respectful of women. She believes that there is a great depth of spirituality to be found in many women who are a part of the women's movement.

Within the Catholic community there are a substantial number of women for whom church means Sunday liturgy only. They value the experience of worshipping God, but they do not see where in Church teachings or practices, their daily experiences and needs are taken into account. These women, often younger women, do not speak out about the need for changes in the Church; they see no point to that. They attend services and pray for God's blessings and understanding.

Secular women's movement activists are puzzled but respectful of the women who actively push and prod the church toward justice for women. The activities chosen vary greatly—a lecture on new ministries for women, a training program for lectors, an organization that educates using feminist theological works, or a national organization advocating and strategizing for the ordination of women.

The women who promote these activities also differ. Some work for an accumulation of smaller gains—first women as lectors or extraordinary ministers of the Eucharist then other changes—; some push to meet a concrete need—more realistic premarital education for the parish's young people. Others see the need for a fundamental reevaluation of the relationship between women and the institutional church. Some hope for rapid change—ordination of women within five years. Others are women who work outside the home, sometimes in Church offices. Many are married, some are women religious, some are single. All know that women have been enriched by the Church and see that, if allowed, they have much to contribute.

The issue of the ordination of women to the priesthood dominates the agenda of a substantial minority of Catholic women. Ordination is an issue in its own right and it has come to symbolize the integration of women into all aspects of Church life. There are many reasons why ordination has become an issue. Women doing pastoral work in hospitals, prisons, and parishes find those they have served many times are unwilling to seek the sacraments from a priest they do not know. If the woman who has ministered to them cannot hear their confession or anoint them, many would rather forego the sacrament. Another reason lies within Church law:

effective decision-making is tied to the authority that comes with ordination. Canon Law excludes all laity (including religious brothers and sisters) from decision-making. This has negative consequences for all, but especially for women who do not share at all in forming Church law or policy.

The question of ordination raises theological and practical questions about the ideas of "call." A "call" to ministry involves an invitation from God to serve and a confirmation of that invitation by the community. Christian churches that have ordained women have done so after deciding that, in fact, women are called. At the present time the Catholic Church denies that women can be called. The ministering that women receive or fail to receive and the relevance or lack thereof to women's lives are also reasons why the issue of ordination is a prominant concern of activist Catholic women.

In 1975, *Pro Mundi Vita,* a European-based research and information center, published a study that puts the activities of U.S. Catholic feminists in a context. In "Women, the Women's Movement, and the Future of the Church," the *Pro Mundi Vita* researchers called attention to new patterns of behavior by European women who identify themselves as Christians. The study points out that traditionally women have carried out the task of "reproducing Christian society by bringing into the world children who they accepted as from the hand of God, and in bringing them up in a Christian fashion, that is to say by transmitting to them the patterns of thinking and acting that were proper to the Church to which they belong." Now there is change.

"To put it concretely, without really knowing why, without any collusion, without premeditation, very many women refuse, more or less unconsciously, to reproduce Christian society in the traditional manner, first, by refusing to give birth to children who they do not want and do not consider as a blessing from God unless they have actually wanted them; and perhaps above all, by no longer educating them according to traditional Christian norms, with the the result that an increasing number of children, not having been educated as Christians by their mothers, or at least not sufficiently, find themselves quickly outside the Church."

The *Pro Mundi Vita* researchers are not talking about activist women. The women's movement within the European Church is very different from that of the United States. It is smaller, more intellectual in its orientation, and more a part of a somewhat larger movement to empower the laity. The movement is not an activists' movement and does not reach most women. Thus, the behavior described by the researchers cannot be attributed to a church-based women's movement, nor, on the basis of the evidence, can it be attributed directly to the secular women's movement. (That movement, too, is still limited in Europe.) The evidence seems to indicate that European women see little hope for change in the Church and are quietly walking away. They have in effect given up on Christianity.

From this perspective, it would seem that the activities of U.S. women, lay and religious, aimed at changing the institutional Church bespeaks hope. Their challenges, demands for change, imply that they expect a positive response to their effort. They look for the institutional church to hear them and enter into dialogue. Some of the hope these women display is plain and simple American optimism: the expectation that with a little goodwill and work any problem can be solved.

This hope, however, is not grounded solely in the United States experience. The women involved, like women worldwide, know the true value of spirituality. They sincerely and deeply appreciate the Church and its traditions. They believe that a Church championing justice in the world will strive to be just itself.

Frustrations

Through history there have been tensions between the authorized leaders of religious communities and the memberships. Most of us know more about the conflicts in the Christian church than those among other religious groups partly because the organizational structures of the church permit some disputes to become public, partly because some of the conflicts have been woven into Western history. We also know that a lot of the stories of struggle have been, if not lost, well buried. This is certainly true of those instances when women were the principal actors. Even so, there is a well-founded feeling that the tensions between women and the Christian churches, especially the Catholic Church, are greater now than they have been in the past. The question—why?

Using the Catholic Church as a case in point: the question can be answered in part by looking at the situation of women, the issues that are the focal point of the tensions, and some of the Church traditions.

Why Now?

Among the many factors that contribute to the tensions between women and the Catholic Church, two seem to stand out: education and knowledge possessed by women and the contradictions between women's actual experiences and needs on the one hand, and on the other, the model of women's life prompted by the Church.

Women in the United States share in the information/knowledge explosion that is now a part of U.S. life. On the whole, women have more formal education today than they did 30 years ago. This is especially true of women religious. The media keep women informed of the advances in the sciences and changes in the society. Slowly the style of questioning and the intellectual skepticism common to the natural sciences have influenced all of life. Women as well as men try to base their behavior on the best knowledge available, enlightened by ethical and religious values.

Today as women question religion they are learning more about their heritage. What was believed to be unchangeable, e.g., priestly celibacy, they find has changed over time. What they thought were well established dogmas of faith, such as the Immaculate Conception, they learn are the relatively recent end products of centuries of thought and popular belief. Equally important, women and men have come to a somewhat better understanding of the interrelationship between culture and faith. They have learned, for example, that the norms of behavior held up to women, the manners and styles of serving, are those of the upper or middle class, certainly not those of the poor or working class. They have also come to appreciate the process of change within the Church. For example, the liturgical changes that were a part of the Vatican Council II were the result of long years of study, dialogue, argument, and experimentation. Much of the latter was not authorized, yet without it no change would have taken place. (The experiences since Vatican II have made clear the need for more thought and experimentation, experimentation with traditional as well as modern styles. Yet for all the criticism few would argue a return to pre-Vatican II practices.)

Because they are knowledgeable, women are becoming active participants in the decisions that affect their lives. They are beginning to trust the validity of their own experiences and judgments. Thus, they are less likely than in the past to unquestioningly accept the directions of the experts, be they doctors or priests.

Too often when tested against knowledge and experience, the stance of the Church with regard to women is found lacking. The models of women and women's life that shapes the Church's approach are no longer accurate. The Church has images of women as either wives or mothers or women religious. (Although it recognizes the calling of singleness, the Church in its practices never seems to see single women.) Women happily take on traditional roles but they know these roles alone do not fully represent them.

First, women are persons; individually they possess a variety of qualities and talents. They are intelligent and are increasingly self-directive.

Relationships shape women's lives. However, if they are to be life-giving, relationships must serve women as well as call women to serve. Women need to be nurtured as well as nurturers. Women need freedom as well as responsibility. They need the opportunities to grow and develop their gifts as well as the duty to encourage and support growth in others.

The life experiences of women vary greatly. Class and race sharply divide women; women of one class or race may not even know of the experience and needs of women in another. The differences in their state of life also separate women. Married women, women religious, and single women have unique responsibilities, life styles, and needs. The growth of common experiences and dialogue among women of different states has bridged some of the differences, yet these are still significant.

The qualities of women, like those of men, also contribute to their differences. Some are risk-takers, others are consolidators. Some are leaders, others followers. There are women who pay attention to details and others who pay attention only to themes. There are women who flourish amidst the constant activities and demands of a large family or a busy office; others do best when quietly and patiently helping a child or adult master a skill; and some do both.

The difference among women are matched by the changes that occur in the life of each woman. Whether married, in religious life, or single, women's concerns and needs shift as they mature. The dreams of the young woman are stripped, reformed, and sometimes held through life. Old women, reflecting on the interplay between dreams and experiences, grow in wisdom.

Women rarely see this mosaic of situations, qualities, and needs expressed in the Church's response to women. Women are not treated as persons, but rather as beings who may be fitted into the role of wife and mother or that of religious. Those who adopt these roles but act them out in a way that reflects their individuality are often marginated. Those who remain single are treated as a product of a social accident or, more often, of their own error. The Church shows some perception of the needs of widows but little of those of divorced or single women. Even those who wholeheartedly embrace the roles of wife and mother or religious find that the institutional Church does not always understand them.

The questions and criticisms women raise are quickly dismissed as inconsequential. Those who persist are labeled troublemakers, misfits, or radicals. Women realize that they are not taken seriously, especially when in response to their questions they are reminded that suffering is a part of the human condition: "We all have a cross to bear."

Many women blame themselves when their experiences do not match Church thinking. They feel guilty and try harder. It is only slowly and painfully that they come to realize that the fault lies not so much in themselves but in the incomplete picture of human society held by churchmen.

There are exceptions to this rather dismal picture. There are parishes and dioceses where women are accepted as full persons. Women have a real voice in decisions; the activities supported mirror the variety of women's interests. These situations are true signs of hope. They are also a witness to the difficulties of incorporating women into the life of the Church. The process, those involved have found, includes not just adding women to decision-making bodies, not just providing new programs, but changing attitudes on the part of the whole community.

The process of changing is still going on even in the parishes that look as if they have successfully incorporated women. It is slow, uneven, sometimes painful. Priests and laity alike must learn how to share in a Church context. Priests especially have a difficult time. Their training (examined in more detail later) does not prepare them to relinquish power nor to relate well to women. Despite these difficulties, those that do change find the experience life giving.

Sources of Frustration

Many issues fuel the discontent of women within the Catholic Church. The four issues looked at below are among the most often cited, a testimony to how important they are to women.

■ Roles of Women.

As married women move into the work force, women religious adopt new ministries, and more women do not marry, the Church's exclusive emphasis on women's role as wife and mother and on the traditional ministries is a source of conflict. In reflection on the question of the proper role of women it is well to keep five facts in mind.

1) Most advocates of a variety of roles for women do not disparage the value of women's traditional roles. They see them as vital and satisfying. But these are not the only roles that should be open to women. In stressing these roles to the extent that it does, the Church in practice contains women within them. The guilt and/or frustration of women who take the Church's dictates to heart is only one consequence of this stress. The Church also reinforces the exclusion of those values and qualities women have nurtured from the civil society.

140

2) Historically, women have had economic as well as child-bearing responsibilities. Although women's production role has received little attention, it has been important to the well-being of family and community and has enhanced women's status. It has also contributed to women's self-esteem. The process of industrialization has ended the production role for middle- and upper-class urban women. However, it has always been a reality of life for working-class and poor women as well as rural women.

3) Most women join the work force out of economic necessity. As the U.S. Labor Department reports, "Nearly two-thirds of all women in the work force in 1978 were single, widowed, divorced or separated, or had husbands whose earnings were less than $10,000 [in 1977]." "In husband-wife families in 1978, 6.1 percent were poor when the wife did not work; 2.7 percent when she was in the labor force." The lower-level standard of living, as proposed by the Labor Department was $11,546 for a family of four in 1978.

4) Not all the qualities and talents women have been endowed with can be developed or exercised if women are solely wives, mothers, or religious in traditional ministries. Women have a responsibility to develop these gifts. When denied the opportunity to do so they and society are poorer.

5) Today, only a small portion of a married woman's lifetime is devoted to full-time childrearing. Once her last child begins school, the child-care demands on a homemaker's time decreases. Most women are still quite young when their children leave home and housekeeping ceases to be a full-time job. If a woman has no other interests but caring for her family, her meaning and self-esteem collapse when her children leave for their own life.

These points and others suggest that it is time for a dialogue between women, church leadership, and theologians so that pastoral practices and theological teachings can take into account the full spectrum of women's lives. Such a dialogue would not minimize the value of the traditional ways of women. It is essential, however, that the institutional Church recognize that women, like men, are too varied to be contained within a few clearly defined roles.

■ **Women, Sexuality, and Marriage.**
Until the post World War II era, secular and Church traditions considered good women to be asexual. Women have known otherwise. Those women who joyfully acknowledged their sexual needs and desires were often labeled evil or felt themselves to be "not good." Most women tended to suppress their sexuality or expressed it only in the context of pregnancy. Recent times have brought a rush of changes. The findings of research into both the psychological and physical aspects of sexuality that began in the

early part of the century have now become a part of the popular culture.

The consequences have been twofold: there has been a great freeing of people's attitudes toward sex; many traditional sex-related values if not being discarded are at least openly questioned.

In examining the tensions that exist between women and the Church on the issues of sexuality, a number of factors stand out.

1) Birth control, pre-marital sex, divorce, and abortion are headline issues but they are not the only and may not be the most basic issues on the agendas. The unspoken underpinnings of many arguments on these issues include a) ideas about patriarchy, conjugal duties, especially those of the wife, and the rights and responsibilities women have over their own body; b) stereotyping women as tempresses or saints; and c) an attitude that women can reach perfection only by becoming male-like. We need to discover how deeply false concepts about women influence our thinking. We need to renew some other concepts such as ideas about conjugal duties and the rights women have over their bodies. Do we, the community called Church, call men and women mutually to conjugal duties, or do we for some reason usually speak of such duties more strongly to women? Why? Do we view the sex-related sins of women as more evil than those of men—to the point of blaming women when their rights over their own body are violated, as for example in rape?

2) Current sexual mores have stimulated research and thought about the values that shape traditional sexual attitudes. The values have strong defenders among those who object to many traditional attitudes and practices. Many, for example, who advocate sex education in the schools firmly hold the need for a moral component in that education, which must be provided by home or church if it cannot be integrated adequately in the school program. Within the love and fidelity of marriage, women as well as men seek to learn more about their own sexuality in order to enjoy more of its pleasures. Women and men are also seeking ways to form and strengthen opposite-sex as well as same-sex friendships because they are aware of the importance of friendships to growth.

Often those who try to strengthen values by incorporating new knowledge into today's attitudes are dismissed because they question traditional views. As a consequence, some give up the effort; others no longer share their insights with the large community.

3) Research evidence is now beginning to back up the perception that women are more sensitive to the impact of their decisions on others than men are. Women are more likely to weigh not only their own interests as they make their choice but also how that choice will affect those with whom they have important relationships. This is especially true of decisions involving intimacy.

142

This approach has been interpreted by some ethicists as a sign of immaturity; women place too much weight on what others think. Others label it as a sham—an excuse to justify a decision. Both responses overlook women's reality and dismiss too quickly a humanizing quality needed for decision-making. From early childhood on females are taught to be concerned about others. "What others will think" is one stage of development. Beyond that lies a realization that one's decisions do impact others' lives— maybe as much as one's own. From this it follows that decisions must involve not only the matter to be decided upon but also the context in which they are to be lived.

The importance of this contextualizing of decision-making should not be overlooked. The difference between what is expected and what is achieved from a decision can often be attributed to a failure to look at the context of the decision. Families are hurt and communities destroyed because someone, a businessman, a government bureaucrat, or a professional expert failed to consider how a decision affected those who had no voice in it.

The institutional Church, like the rest of society, fails to realize the place relationships have in women's decision-making. This is particularly painful for women when sexuality and life in marriage are the issues being decided upon.

4) For Catholic women, freedom of conscience is a difficult issue. Vatican II and other official Church statements sanction persons' rights to form their own conscience and then act. The right is not without limits. Persons and communities have the responsibility of informing themselves of the teachings of the Church and making their decisions in the light of these teachings.

The encyclical *Humanae Vitae* has proved to be a testing place for Catholic women. Some women could and did accept the Church's ban on the use of artificial contraception. Others could not. In time these women have either justified their continued use of artificial birth control by citing the Church's teachings on freedom of conscience or they have left the Church. Many others felt that they were caught between a rock and a hard place. The stakes included their marriage, their family's well-being, the dreams of a lifetime, religious fidelity, and a sense of sin. Some of these women have never resolved the question for themselves. They cannot justify their continued use of contraceptives by citing freedom of conscience and live with a destructive sense of guilt. For most women the decision was painful, tentative, and filled with guilt. They were disillusioned and alienated by the way the decision was reached.

Today, many women still find decisions about birth control difficult to make although they bring more confidence to that decision. *Humanae Vitae* remains a major source of conflict between women and the Church. (Married men, too, have found *Humanae Vitae* a hard issue, but most seem confident and at peace with their response.) It symbolizes the Church's failure to appreciate the reality of women's lives and the contradictions in Church teachings.

Women have had no voice in decisions that affect the core of their being. Pope Paul VI made the decision on banning artificial means of birth control. He was supported in that decision by a hierarchy who, like himself, had too frequently been cut off from women and their ordinary concerns. This is the historic pattern of Church decision-making.

Would the decisions be the same if women had a voice in them? The answer can only be guessed at. It is worth noting, however, that life and death issues that have touched men's lives have frequently been nuanced in Church teachings. The just war theory, arguments about self-defense, and the principles of double effect have been explored and developed around life and death issues that men face. The development of these theories established principles that allowed men to engage in morally ambiguous activities under some circumstances. The life and death issues that women face have not always been so carefully nuanced. Would, for example, Church teachings about birth control be any different if principles dealing with the context of the decision—a significant part of women's moral decision-making process described earlier—were incorporated?

6) Different approaches to the moral development of young people place unfair burdens on young women and foster irresponsibility among young men. Girls, for example, are told while still very young that they are responsible for their own sexuality and that of their male friends as well. Boys receive the message that they have less responsibility for their behavior, in effect because they are less able to control themselves. This double standard covers a wide range of areas including language, attitudes towards one's own body, and norms of modesty. Different sets of norms make it difficult for individual men and women to understand each other's behavior. More importantly, it makes it much more difficult for men and women to develop norms for sexual behavior that demonstrate maturity and mutual responsibility.

■ The Image of God.

Catholics, female and male, learn early in their lives that they and all people are created in the image and likeness of God. While this is not denied, theology and practice has in effect stressed the maleness of God. An example of this is the *Declaration on Question* of the *Admission of Women to the Ministerial Priesthood* released in January, 1977. In arguing why women cannot be priests the declaration states "there would not be this 'natural resemblance' which must exist between Christ and His minister if the role of Christ is not taken by a man." The argument continues and in effect claims that the male physical sexuality is an important element in sacramentally imaging Christ. The declaration stresses Christ's maleness rather than his humanity. Since the Council of Chalcedon in the Fifth Century the Church has taught that "What is not assumed [by Christ] is not yet redeemed."

The declaration raises serious questions. Is maleness an essential character in Christ? If it is can Christ have represented women who do not bear that essential character in his crucifixion and death? Are women redeemed?

For Catholic women who have been exploring the question of the ordination of women the declaration has been a serious source of anguish as well as anger. The Pontifical Biblical Commission found that nothing in the New Testament forbids the ordaining of women. To many, this finding removed a significant barrier to women's ordination. Then the declaration was released, making dialogue between women and the hierarchy much more difficult.

To date the hierarchy has not seemed to hear the difficulties women face because of the declaration. And the question remains, if women cannot image Christ are they created in the image of God? Are they saved?

■ Sexist Language.

As women grow more self-conscious about being women, they begin to hear in new ways. The lack of balance in language begins to grate. Women have a deeply felt sense that they are usually not included, protestations to the contrary notwithstanding, in the expression "man . . . he . . . . " Experience has taught women that mankind does not mean all humankind but rather male human beings.

The question of balanced language in the Church is an especially frustrating and angering one. Unlike so many issues of tension between women and the Church, implementing the use of balanced language in many situations is possible without the approval of the hierarchy or the Vatican. Only changes in the language of the Mass and other liturgical Rites need the official action of the Church. In other instances, all that is required is simple awareness and a little forethought on the part of individuals.

Linguists have found that language does shape our thoughts and perceptions. For example, most adults and children picture God as male. One can test how deeply ingrained this perception is by watching the reaction when someone refers to God as she or mother. Some object; almost everyone is uncomfortable. Yet if we believe what we claim—that God is neither male nor female—it should be just as appropriate to refer to God as she as it is to say he.

Anthropologists tell us that we can learn a lot about ranking in a society just by listening for who is and is not addressed. The failure to use balanced language says much about the status of women in the Church.

Three points need to be made in order to answer the question that arises with regard to balanced language.

1) In some languages, there is a commonly used distinct word meaning all persons, human beings, and another word for men plus a word for women. Latin is one such language. The word *homo* means "person." *Vir* means "man"; *mulier* means "woman." Thus, in many instances a translation into English that does use inclusive language is truer to the original than the use of man when "person" or "human being" is intended.

2) There are instances where the use of human being, person, or people might not be proper. But there are not very many. Biblical scholars, for example, admit that the word "man" has been used in many instances when person would be as appropriate. Still, most advocates of balanced language are not asking that basic documents be changed—unless they have been charged already, e.g., spiritual classics that have been "modernized" many times. Some hymns cannot easily be changed although writers and publishers have succeeded in rewording many. The Eucharistic liturgy needs hierarchical approval for change. The number of instances like this are small, however, and do not mean that no changes should be made.

3) The use of balanced language is not going to scandalize, alienate, or otherwise disturb those who are not yet sensitive to its importance. It may, in fact, infuse more meaning into liturgical celebration by changing what often sounds abstract into the concrete of daily life. Sermons that speak of men and women, and informal prayers and hymns that are inclusive in language can only enrich our spiritual life.

Barriers to Change

Tradition, more than faith and morals, stands in the way of more just treatment of women in the Church. There are theological issues to be examined and explored. These, although very important, do not match in scope or weight the traditions of 20 centuries.

How are we to act? Why are things the way they are? What is the proper behavior? To answer these and similar questions we look to tradition to answer.

Tradition is difficult to deal with. It is filled with contradictions. On the one hand it enriches and humanizes, on the other hand it limits and stunts. Church traditions are no different than other traditions. By fleshing out the teachings of the Church, tradition makes them more real in the lives of people. The stories, myths, and practices handed on from generation to generation, have given meaning to the events of daily life and cause for celebration.

But tradition is also bound. It is related to a place, a time, and a history. It is built upon the knowledge of its time.

When tradition is not open to being reinterpreted in the light of new knowledge it either fragments or becomes defensive. Church traditions have experienced both. Defensiveness has grown around the tradition related to women. And because they are traditions handed down by a faith community those who question them are viewed as challenging religion. Yet questions of women's roles, behavior, rights, and responsibilities in the society are better answered in today's world by referring to the situation of women rather than tradition. Our traditions were built during a time when village life revolved around the seasons. Theology and spirituality are important components of our life but so are the findings of economics, sociology, and psychology.

We need tradition. We need the sense of continuity and rootedness that tradition conveys. We need its values to humanize our lives. But we need that tradition to deal with our real world. A tradition that sees women as overgrown children, passive, unlearned, good only for menial services, does not minister to women or to our society.

Our times call on us to dialogue with our traditions, to ask new questions, to separate the essence from its time-bound dress. Few women in our society spin or weave but many are engaged in other kinds of productive work. Can we sanction these new activities as we did spinning, weaving, and farming? There is less need today for women to clean and sweep the Church, wash and iron the linen. But there is a need for lectors, and hospital and prison chaplains. Can we adapt our traditions to encompass these roles?

Our tradition tells us little about the holy women of the past. Can we move them from the margins so that their truth and wisdom might enrich us? Feminine spirituality is beginning to grow. Can we draw on our traditions to both nurture and challenge it so that it becomes not a passing fad but a genuine expression of human seeking and growth?

■ Priestly Formation.

If our traditions are to grow and continue to nourish us it is essential that the education and experiences of our priests change. The common pattern of priestly formation separates young men from the rest of the community, and especially from women, for an extended period of time. During a period of life when both men and women are maturing, these young men are virtually isolated from women except for housekeepers and family. They experience their own growth and development, but they have little occasion to appreciate the same growth in women. Even those students who do have occasion to have more contact with women, because of their seminary experience, tend to approach women in a paternalistic manner.

Once priests are ordained a substantial number still have little occasion to develop respect for and understanding of women. They meet a few women as authority figures and some as individuals to be indulged, the housekeeper for example. Most women they meet seek their counselling. Some are secretaries or in similar subordinate positions. Many priests do not know women as peers. They are unwilling to recognize that the knowledge, experiences, and judgments of women are on a par with or superior to their own and must be taken seriously. Others come to recognize women's capabilities and are intimidated.

The isolation increases for those men who move into and up through the Church bureaucracy. They have even less occasion to know about the life of the ordinary woman. Insulation adds to isolation. Respectful of "Father," many women refuse to question or in any way be assertive with a priest. In effect they adopt the oriental practice of telling the person in authority what he wants to hear.

In this fictional environment priests and bishops usually come to expect a certain passive diffidence from the women around them. Strong women who are willing to challenge them are threatening. If such women cannot be avoided they are labeled—angry, opinionated, unfeminine, disobedient—and their ideas about the relationship between women and the Church dismissed.

The consequences of this situation are disastrous for all involved. Training, personal regard for the individuals they work with, and sometimes the necessity to keep a job lead most women working with clergy to be deferential toward them. Some protest their psyche and achieve their personal goals by manipulating their boss, as women in restrictive cultures have manipulated men through time—hardly a Christ-like situation. Some women work within the Church knowing that the day will come when frustration and anger will force them to end that work. They hope they can accomplish some good in the interim. If women's alienation is so great that they leave the Church, they are defined as unfaithful—again the victim made to bear the blame.

Clergy continue in their isolation. They have little if any appreciation of the experiences, values, and styles of women. Too often, priests and bishops alike, disdain women! Silly women, castrating women, nunny bunny, neurotic, are not uncommon categories clerics have for women.

The tensions and divisions between women and the institutional Church grow. And the community of the faithful suffers.

Meeting the Challenge of the Future

The changes in the world's societies present significant challenges to all religions. Changes in global economic and political structures are affecting the relationships among nations and among people. Yet, the age-old questions remain: Who is God? How do I love God? Who is my neighbor? How do I love my neighbor? The answers, however, seem more complicated than in the past.

In the hurried, complex environment of an industrialized society it seems more difficult to find God. Many Christians are learning it is not enough to be persons of good will in order to do what seems to be God's will. They find themselves in situations where the alternatives appear to be equally unchristian if not evil. The world grows in interdependence and we are beginning to realize that our neighbor on the other side of the world and on the other side of town have much in common. The better life both seek influences our lives. They ask that we share our resources including our power. It is not always easy to respond.

The mixed blessings of our technology also raise old questions in new ways for different societies. The mass media, bringing new knowledge into our homes, has helped us understand our world. But, it also brings values that could at one time be quarantined. How, for example, do U.S. parents respond to the increasing sensationalizing of sex that is so pervasive in our society?

The women's issue demonstrates the complexity of the challenge facing all religions including Catholicism. This issue is also one of many that suggest the same response; the emergency of a Church that is rooted in the local culture and finds its expression in local experiences.

The needs of women in India are very different from those of Latin America or the United States. In India the Church must convince women they are loved by God and have worth in a society where poverty robs many of dignity. In Latin America there is the question of empowering women in a macho society, where women have much responsibility but little authority. This issue is particularly important to the Church because a significant number of women are serving in place of priests as parish ministers. In the U.S., we are struggling with questions of personhood, equality, and participation, questions that arise with force in a post-industrial society.

The concept of a universal Church that is united yet rooted in the local culture is both attractive and practical. Theologians and others who have begun to explore the idea see in it the possibility of recognizing and responding to the uniqueness of the local community while preserving the unity that has been a mark of the Catholic Church. In such a Church people could probe their own reality and come to understand better what it means to be a Christian in that culture. The insights and understanding gained would be shared and critiqued by the whole Church and would contribute to building the Kingdom. There would be differences in liturgies and other practices, reflecting local culture, but unity in faith and love.

In a Church rooted in the local cultures the situation of women would be better understood and more easily wrestled with. In the U.S. Church, the dialogue that women have sought with Church leaders could proceed. Specific issues, not at this time concerns of the Church universal, could be jointly reflected upon. Tradition, Church practices, and culture could be questioned from the perspective of women's experiences. Women in turn could be challenged by tradition and the rest of the Church community.

Equally important, an "indigenous Church" would be free to acknowledge and respond to the vast differences that exist among U.S. women. Usually women see the Church leadership recognizing only two sets of experiences: those of the traditional roles of wife and mother, as experienced by middle-class women, or that of women religious. Yet Catholic women reflect the pluralism that marks our society.

Recognition of that pluralism by the Church as a whole would be an important step to strengthening the people of God. Women whose experiences and life style do not fit into traditional molds would no longer feel alienated. A variety of organizations with differing interests and styles might develop, and women with different life experiences would not be struggling for some access to influence the hierarchy's thinking.

The styles that are a part of U.S. culture could also be handled more easily by a Chruch community rooted in its own culture. For example, dissent is a highly respected aspect of U.S. life but it is not a characteristic of Church life. When Americans respond to Church policy by dissenting, the leadership becomes very defensive. A Church rooted in the U.S. experience would soon find itself at ease dealing with public questioning and criticism. Meetings and vigils would be recognized as an effort on the part of people to be heard.

It goes without saying that there are areas of Church life not open to dissent: our basic faith heritage, "the deposit of faith and its authentic interpretation." The legitimization of dissent will require that all of us, bishop, priest, and people look more carefully at that faith heritage and carefully distinguish the authentic deposit of faith from cultural additions. This will enable us to create ways of expressing our faith that are appropriate to our times.

The suggestions outlined above are not utopian. Activities and processes are underway that are showing what a rooted Church might look like. Some of the experiences of those involved in the women's movement within the Church are examples of what might happen. The four cases sketched below illustrate what is happening now.

■ Women Bonding.

Ten years ago lay women and women religious were virtually mysteries to each other. Individuals in one state of life had a friend who lived the other, and they agreed their lives had little in common. In the intervening time there have been significant changes. Women in different states of life are working together. They are exploring common problems, and cooperating on joint projects. They are sharing insights and resources and offering each other support. This new sense of cooperation is cutting across class, racial, and geographic barriers. There may well be, for example, more sharing among Hispanic and Anglo women on Church-related issues than on any other.

This bonding process has not been easy. Misconceptions and negative attitudes have had to be overcome. Women have had to look deeply into themselves, recognize past hurts, and put them into perspective. Someone has had to identify the common interest. Women have had to listen with new ears. The results have been well worth the effort, however. In many communities women from different backgrounds understand each other better, work for common causes, and nurture rewarding friendships.

■ Women in Ministry.

Over the last 10 years the two post-Vatican II changes in the Church have come together. The definition of ministry has expanded, at least in practice, to encompass many of the ways the people of God serve each other and the community at large. In addition, the Church community has been enriched by more women doing more different jobs. As a consequence of these two changes there has been renewed interest in what it means to minister and also a growth in women's consciousness of restraints they face within Church institutions. (The growth of women in ministry has been a factor in the bonding among lay women and women religious.) The involvement of more women in ministerial positions has, moreover, stimulated research and new questions.

The latter, in particular, grow as women begin studying theology in order to be better ministers. Although the issue of ordination of women has a longer history (the St. Joan's Alliance, established in 1911 in London to promote the equality of women, began advocating the ordination of Roman Catholic women in 1963), it is now an integral part of the ministry question. Self-confident in their feminism, many women bring determination and fresh insights to the probing of these questions.

In 1978, the Leadership Conference of Women Religious (LCWR) initiated a study: Women and Ministry. The LCWR decided on the study after listening to the many questions raised by women in ministry, surveying the available data, and coming to the conclusion that the information on hand would not answer the questions posed. Rather than define precise ministerial roles, the study began by identifying a set of criteria that if met would identify a particular activity as ministry. The criteria included motivation, service, and social context, as well as other factors. The finds of the study show that 95 percent of the women doing work that meets the criteria are lay women. It also shows that in addition to serving in new roles such as lectors, Eucharistic Ministers and retreat workers, women are continuing to fill traditional roles, such as maintaining and decorating the altar, secretarial work, and religious education instructors.

The evaluation of a rooted Church would facilitate the growth of lay ministry in a direction that would further enrich and strengthen the U.S. church.

■ New Theologies.

Conversation with women and men, lay, religious, and clerical indicates the need to develop together theologies that respond to today's needs. Questions about family and work are high on the list. In addition, women, in particular, are asking that the people of God look afresh at Mary, her life and her role in the life of the Church. These are not solely "women's issues" yet they are of great importance to women, and women's contributions are vital if these theologies are to meet today's needs.

In the United States as in the rest of the industrial world, the relationship between the work many people do and the needs of people is hidden. An increasing number of Americans no longer directly work to produce food, shelter, or essential clothing. Many see no connection between their work and these basic needs. Why, then, do we need work? Just to make money? How? This is just one set of questions, with theological as well as economic implications long facing men but now facing women as well. How do we, who call ourselves Christians, bring together our faith and our work life? How do the Church's social teachings fit into today's technology-dominated work world? Do businesses have a social responsibility other than making money?

The occasions for forming renewed theology of family are at hand. The U.S. Bishops Pastoral Plan of Action for the Family and the 1980 Synod of Bishops will generate some of the material out of which this theology can be constructed. The women's movement in both Church and society has raised some of the issues that must be examined. And the theology is developing.

Marriage Encounter, Catholic Family Movement, and Christian Life Communities, are just three national organizations that are probing the lived experiences of Catholic couples. Each of these groups has its own perspectives, goals, and agenda. Within these groups couples are confronting the issues raised by our society and the women's movement. They are reflecting on the variations in relationships between men and women and their consequences. These groups would welcome the opportunity to share their questions and insights with the Church as a whole. They have much to contribute to a renewed theology of marriage, especially one that takes seriously the United States experience.

Since Vatican II devotion to Mary has waned. Young people in particular have found Mary interesting but not especially relevant to their lives. Younger women have turned from Mary. They saw in the Marian stories and devotion a rationale for keeping women out of the mainstream of life. The characteristics of Mary that have been praised are those that have contributed to the powerlessness of women. Mary became a symbol for passivity, unreasonable patience, the pedestal that removed women from real life.

This turn from Mary, however, has been only half-hearted; women have felt that if they had a voice in telling the story, it might well be different. In a sense, women have resented having to "give up" Mary, yet they have been unwilling to accept the old model. Recently some new ways of looking at Mary that have relevance to our times have begun to emerge! Mary as refugee in Egypt; Mary who followed her migrant son. These new perspectives have been accompanied by a renewed appreciation of the decisions that marked her life. Mary's openness to God as the young woman of the Annunciation; her faithfulness at the Cross. The Magnificat is recognized as a powerful statement proclaiming the justice of God:

> He has shown the power of his arm,
> He has routed the proud of heart.
> He has pulled down princes from their
>   thrones and exalted the lowly.
> The hungry He has filled with good
>   things, the rich sent empty away.

Women and men, together, are reexamining Mary and her life in the light of today's experiences. Perhaps those facets of Mary's life that appeal most to people in the United States will not immediately capture the imagination of people in other parts of the Church. But it is needed by U.S. women. It is needed by the U.S. Church dedicated to Mary. And it will contribute to building the people of God.

■ New Styles of Worship.

As in other times, the needs of people living today are calling forth new styles of worship. Through the ages, Mass has been the central act of worship for Catholics. However, the large, often anonymous Sunday Mass has seemed to many as just another example of our impersonal society. Parishes and groups within parishes have responded by forming small communities. These communities, sometimes neighborhood based, meet regularly for liturgy and sharing. They have proved to be an effective vehicle for building intimacy and support while deepening the faith of those participating.

These small community meetings, which are evolving into a North American version of the Latin American base community, have often but not always involved a Eucharistic liturgy. With time and experience, groups have developed prayer services that have been faith building. Instead of Eucharist, the liturgy may be organized around biblical readings, prayers, and faith sharing. These communities also provide an occasion for women to shape and lead liturgy, thereby giving women the opportunity to develop styles of worship that reflect women's approach to God and their interpretation of the concerns of the community.

These smaller communities can contribute significantly to the building of a rooted Church. They provide the opportunity, not possible at Sunday Mass, for people to examine their own experiences in the light of the Bible and the Church teachings. They also nurture the supportive relationships that are often missing from our modern, technical society.

The women's movement has raised many questions for religion. Women who are aware of the injustice they and others face recognize that religious institutions contribute to those injustices. At the same time, they are very appreciative of the spiritual value religions have nurtured and the importance of these values to themselves and to all women. Women have great hope. They believe that religious institutions can be just. And like the Canaanite woman who pestered Jesus, they will continue to pester religious institutions. The Canaanite woman's daughter was cured. Women expect that sexism can be cured.

Suggested Readings

Walter Burkhardt, S.J., ed. *Women: New Dimensions* (Paulist Press, New York, 1977).
Essays that explore issues of women and church with the aim of furthering theological thinking about women.

Carol Gilligan "In a Different Voice: Women's Concepts of Self and Morality," *Harvard Educational Review* (Vol. 47, No. 4, November 1977). Using the context of women making decisions about abortion, this article explores the importance of relationships in women's decision-making.

Rosemary Ruether, *New Woman/New Earth* (The Seabury Press, New York, 1975).
Theological reflections on some aspects of women's past leading to an analysis of changes needed to build a just future.

Rachel Conrad Wahlberg, *Jesus According to Women* (Paulist Press, New York, 1975).
A very readable fresh look at some familiar Gospel stories that leads to theologizing from a feminist perspective.

7.
CONCLUSION

The women's movement and the United States look forward to the last decades of the century with a mixture of feelings. Hope and fear are intertwined. The nation hopes that the answers to the questions of the 1960s and 1970s will finally emerge. An end to the uncertainty about energy and to inflation are high on people's agenda. Security, material and psychic, is a priority.

The U.S. Women's Movement, strongly rooted in our society, shares in this hope. Women want the gains they have won in the fields of employment and legal rights to spread through all sectors of the society. Understanding and acceptance of the movement are primary goals.

Fears temper hope. The answers the nation seeks are complex. They call for more changes: changes in our style of living and in our expectations. Changes are not necessarily bad. Most of us say we would welcome a growth of interest in the common good, or of living better with fewer material goods. But many of us are also tired of change, any change, and will resist it mightily. Witness our reluctance to change our driving habits, for example, or in other ways conserve energy. We want to promote the common good but frequently think of it as the good of those who share our life style. Living better with less is usually seen as less for others, for we need the new appliance, the new equipment.

The women's movement, too, has its fears, some of which are shared by the wider justice-seeking community. There is fear, for example, that in the reaction against change efforts will be made to turn back the gains made by women. There is concern that in despair about the complexity of the issues we face, people will choose authoritarian solutions that are simplistic and unjust. Families face new and difficult challenges, for example, but public and private policies that force most women to become full-time homemakers will not reduce these challenges and may in fact complicate them further.

Reasons for Hope

The women's movement's hopes are well grounded. The movement can cite with pride some important accomplishments. The

156

struggle of women for their rights is a justice issue involving basic human rights. That principle is not yet fully established; nevertheless, more and more men and women accept it as true and are trying to give it meaning in their lives.

Twenty years ago when women and men concerned about social values talked about the gifts of women they had a common catalogue to quote from. Women humanized our society we were told. Few noted that this humanization occurred only in the home, not the larger society. Today when we talk of women's gifts we speak of the great variety of abilities and virtues that women exercise in the public sphere as well as the home. We have come to realize, as well, that men do not fit into neat categories.

In making us aware of the many different talents of women, the women's movement has freed women and men to nurture all their gifts and grow. Men and women have been able to try new activities: today in the U.S. there are women miners and men homemakers. We are still testing gender roles in our society. We do not know how deeply ingrained our attitudes are. We do not know if and to what extent biology does limit roles. We are testing both attitudes and capabilities. In the process we have created tensions and psychic insecurity. Some—young women especially—find themselves with choices that they are almost afraid to make. Yet for all of this, women are finding that the new freedoms they have grasped are life giving. Once the first painful steps are taken women do not want to return to old ways. Men are finding that the new ways may mean sharp, even painful, changes but they do lead to a richer, more whole life.

The gains made because of the women's movement are not all abstract. Men are more involved in child care and household responsibilities than in the past. Children and parents both benefit, especially the men who build stronger relationships with their children. The children, too, seem to be happier, growing in new ways.

Women in the work force are receiving equal pay for equal work, but most women are still segregated into low-paying jobs. Even so, a greater variety of positions are open to women and men. More women are being better educated. Women lawyers and doctors are on the rise. However, much must still be done. Parking meter repairmen earn more than registered nurses. There are few women in tenured positions in colleges and universities. Women in positions of power in business are rare.

Women are meeting the needs of women and men in many different settings. There are women ministers and rabbis. Within the Catholic community, women have responded to the community's new requisites by fashioning new ministries: nuns are community organizers, mothers are directors of religious education. Women, through new organizations, are helping women cope with the trauma of divorce and widowhood, and the readjustments homemakers face when all the children leave home. Some of those who have taken on these new roles insist that their decisions have not been infuenced by the women's movement. There is truth in this, for the same societal pressures that have fashioned the women's movement have created the needs these women see and respond to.

Women have begun to change their relationships with the medical profession. They are asking doctors harder questions. They are demanding that research be extended to deal with their needs in a better way. Surgery, cancer treatment, and other medical procedures are being reevaluated because some pushy women have insisted that the medical profession be more accountable to women.

The list grows as under the impetus of the women's movement new attitudes about women open new opportunities to them. Women look upon each other with greater respect. Women are searching through family history, religious history, and national history to learn more about the lives of women in the past. And all of us are being enriched.

Causes of Fear

As there are grounds for hope within the women's movement, there are grounds for fear. Some are rooted in the limits of the movement and the mistakes of the past. Few black, Hispanic, and other minority women identify with the movement per se. Many are strong and effective advocates of one or another issue that the movement struggles for, equal pay for equal work, for example, or shelters and other help for battered women. But it is difficult for many of these women to identify themselves with a movement whose public leaders embody a style and a set of values that has no place in their lives. There is seldom room in the lives of minority women for the anger at men that some middle-class white women have experienced. Minority women share with minority men the weight of racism and that oppression seems, at this time, heavier than sexism. If the women's movement is to reach its potential, minority women must be reached and honestly incorporated into the movement.

As the impact of sexism becomes more clear, a growing number of minority women are finding that the women's movement does speak for them. Equally important, they are finding that, slowly, white women within the movement are beginning to appreciate the evils of racism.

Those poor women who have the time and energy to be aware of the women's movement see many issues on its agenda as luxuries. These same women have been threatened by some stances of the movement because their needs have been overlooked. Some of the working poor, for example, are working as domestics for women who have fought and finally gained better pay and working conditions for themselves. These same women pay the women working for them minimal wages and often subject them to poor working conditions. It is difficult for these poor working women to imagine the women's movement will change their lives for the better.

The movement is becoming more knowledgeable about the situation of women in all sectors of our society. Coalitions, which included welfare women, and working poor women as well as women's organizations are being formed to deal with specific needs—e.g., the working conditions in a specific plant, the needs of the elderly, or the educational needs of women. These coalitions though small in number are opening the women's movement to the need of many who cannot yet speak out for themselves. They are also helping poor women gain needed skills and resources.

Much of the early attention to the Women's Movement focused on its denial of traditional values and practices. Women who belonged to the movement condemned marriage, questioned the value of children, criticized religion. Fidelity in marriage was identified as a trap. Homemaking was disparaged. Women who filled that role were often treated as inferiors. Divorce rates climbed, as did abortion rates.

We are finding however that all the criticism and condemning has involved something more than a rejection of past values. For some women, it has been just that: rejection. For many others, however, it has been part of the effort of creating space for change for themselves and others. The familial and social ties that bound these women were too tight. In order to make choices other than the conventional, to choose values that differed from those promoted by society they had to tear at the old. There seemed no other way.

Having created the space needed to examine anew old values and the institutions that carried them, feminists are reevaluating some past stances. Increasingly values are affirmed but past expressions of those values are challenged. Younger women who have options because of past struggles are asserting the value of close and faithful relationships. Children are recognized as a prime good. The importance of loving child care is acknowledged, and supported by women who once rejected these values. Together these women are searching for ways to live out traditional values in a manner that treats women fairly.

The challenges to the old ways arise not only from the women's movement but from the society itself. Families are smaller. Women who are mothers are also in the work force. Women who devoted themselves to homemaking find themselves alone in their 50s because of widowhood or divorce with many years of healthy life ahead of them.

Although the U.S. women's movement recognizes that it is a part of a global movement, it knows little of the issues before women in many parts of the world. There are U.S. feminists who are deeply involved in the global effort for equality for women, but they are relatively few and with the exception of Gloria Steinem are not nationally known. Some of these women spend some of their time informing more women about the similarities and differences of needs that exist among women worldwide. United Nations meetings, professional meetings, conferences on specific issues help spread information. But this aspect of the women's movement still needs to be developed.

Commonly held attitudes about the relationships with other nations, the size of the United States, the diversity of its population, and the rightful human tendency to deal with issues close at hand make it difficult for the US. Women's Movement to become more integrated into a global movement. Nevertheless, the U.S. movement has much influence within the global movement. It serves as a model for organization and action. It can influence U.S. policies that affect women in other nations.

There would be benefits for U.S. women if the movement's agenda were placed within the context of a global movement. Women would, for example, discover the variety of ways women have constructed to balance the demands of family and community with their own responsibilities and interests. They would also come to a better understanding of the social and economic structures that shape our lives. A new perspective and many new insights would help achieve a more just society here and worldwide.

There is still much to be done if women are to be treated justly and if the process is to contribute to a just world. First, the U.S. movement must continue the effort to overcome the limits by which it is now framed. The attempt to include women who are black, Hispanic, members of other minority groups, Asians and Native Americans, for example, will need to be more vigorous. A lot more attention needs to be given to the concerns of women in other parts of the world. The cooperation that can follow will do much to create a more just society for all.

The second set of tasks, like that above, is already underway. We need to identify values that are essential to a human and just society, separate these values from practices that no longer serve us, and find ways to express them today.

The renewed interest in family life on the part of feminist organizations is one indication that this set of tasks is being taken seriously. It is not enough, however, to reassert the importance of family life. There is a need to institute styles of family life that will enable families to thrive in today's environment. Communications within families is one key. Can the women's movement facilitate such communication? Women have developed styles of decision-making that are more consensual and less authoritarian and at least as effective as past models. Some families have already begun to use these models. Can ways be found to help more families investigate these styles and adapt them to their needs? What are the support systems needed by the nuclear family, the single-parent family, the extended family? Can the women's movement contribute to structuring these systems? Are there viable forms of family life other than the nuclear family? What would they be? How would they express the fundamental values of love, security, respect for differences? How would they meet the challenges of a technological society? What would they need to better meet those challenges? What's the worth of household work? Child care? How does the work contribute to the family? To the society? How can it be given the recognition it deserves? These are just a few of the value-laden questions about family life that the women's movement must help answer.

Work has been on the movement's agenda for many years. As one issue is resolved new questions arise. Why, for example, has the wage gap between men and women grown despite increased numbers of women in better paying jobs and "equal pay" laws? Does it have something to do with the fact that 80 percent of all women working outside the home work in "women's jobs?" Is "women's work" less valuable to the society? If not, should not women be paid equal with men for work of equal value? If women are paid wages equal to men for work that is as valuable to the employer as men's work what will this mean for the economy? For family life? For women's role in society? Might it not lead to a more just society? If women were paid fairly for the work they do outside the home would it not ease many financial problems families face? Might it not open the way for men and women both to work shorter work weeks freeing them to spend more time with the family? These questions, high on the agenda of the women's movement, need answers drawn from the experiences of many women.

Power scares many women. Yet if women are going to contribute to reshaping society they must have power. The questions abound. What is power? Should women have power? How should they exercise it? Can it be exercised in only one way or can it be manifested in many ways? Power over what? Can it be shared? How?

If these and similar value questions are going to be answered to the benefit of all, the answer-seeking must involve all. Openness to dialogue is a challenge not only to the women's movement but to all women. Dialogue will not erase differences. It will not even make differences understandable to everyone. Dialogue will, however, surface the fragments which then will have to be tested and fitted together to form viable responses to vital questions.

Finally, if we are to build societies that are just to women and men alike, we are going to have to reexamine our basic concepts of what it means to be human, to be man, to be woman, what persons do, what women do, what men do. We will need to look at our basic concepts not just as they are expressed in our economic system and our laws but as they shape us through our religious beliefs and our culture. The task is a long, difficult, and sensitive one. It will question the values we hold dear. We will find contradictions; contradictions between individual women's beliefs and experiences, contradictions between the experiences in different situations. The prospect of examining these basic issues is threatening for women who often do not have the resources to live with more changes. These women must be respected as well as supported as new ideas are examined and tested.

The need for this task of examining our basic concepts of what it means to be woman and man is clear. Women are full persons, their contributions to society are important. Words are used to tell women how important they are but when women try to translate the words into meeting their needs or those of their families the words become meaningless. It is clear that we carry within us some ideas about women and men that prevent us from seeing real persons, living real lives. If we are to change our society so that women and men alike are to be truly human it is time we begin exposing these inhibiting attitudes.

The women's movement has reached a healthy adolescence. Its limits and failures are evident. Its accomplishments are also clear. It has nudged and pulled us on the first steps of a long road toward a just society. If that goal is to be reached we must all be both critics and supporters.